DK EYEWITNESS

TOP 10
AZORES

Top 10 Azores Highlights

Welcome to the Azores.................**5**
Exploring the Azores......................**6**
Azores Highlights.........................**10**
Ponta Delgada.............................**12**
Caldeira das Sete Cidades **14**
Whale and Dolphin
    Watching **16**
Vale das Furnas...........................**18**
Angra do Heroísmo......................**20**
Diving Spots................................**24**
Horta..**26**
Capelinhos..................................**28**
Algar do Carvão **30**
Paisagem da Cultura da
    Vinha da Ilha do Pico...............**32**

The Top 10 of Everything

Moments in History **36**
Churches and Chapels **38**
Museums.....................................**40**
Natural Wonders.........................**42**
Natural Swimming Pools
    and Thermal Springs...............**44**
Walks and Hikes **46**
Outdoor Activities.......................**50**
Birdlife **52**
Traditional Azorean
    Cuisine **54**
Restaurants................................**56**
Places to Shop **58**
Arts and Crafts............................**60**
Traditional Festivals....................**62**

CONTENTS

Azores Area by Area

São Miguel and Santa
Maria Islands.............................**66**

Terceira and Graciosa
Islands.......................................**76**

São Jorge, Pico and
Faial Islands.............................**88**

Flores and Corvo Islands............**98**

Streetsmart

Getting Around **106**

Practical Information................**108**

Places to Stay............................**112**

General Index **118**

Acknowledgments **124**

Phrase Book...............................**126**

Within each Top 10 list in this book, no hierarchy of quality or popularity is implied. All 10 are, in the editor's opinion, of roughly equal merit.

Title page, front cover and spine *The picturesque Poço do Bacalhau, Flores Island* ***Back cover, clockwise from top left*** *Colourful marine life; the harbour at Angra do Heroísmo; Portas da Cidade; Poço do Bacalhau; the town of Angra do Heroísmo*

The rapid rate at which the world is changing is constantly keeping the DK Eyewitness team on our toes. While we've worked hard to ensure that this edition of Azores is accurate and up-to-date, we know that opening hours alter, standards shift, prices fluctuate, places close and new ones pop up in their stead. So, if you notice we've got something wrong or left something out, we want to hear about it. Please get in touch at **travelguides@dk.com**

Welcome to
The Azores

The nine islands of the Azores, scattered in the Atlantic Ocean, are noted for their biodiversity and offer a wealth of outdoor and adventure tourism options. The archipelago is also packed with historical and cultural charm. These islands have something for everyone, and with DK Eyewitness Top 10 Azores, they're yours to explore.

Clustered into three areas – the Eastern Group duo of **São Miguel** and **Santa Maria**, the Central Group quintet of **Terceira**, **Graciosa**, **São Jorge**, **Pico** and **Faial**, and the Western Group pairing of **Flores** and **Corvo** – these islands differ widely. The Azores' volcanic origins are evident in the massive **Sete Cidades** crater and soaring **Montanha do Pico** – Portugal's highest mountain. **Capelinhos** volcano is a reminder of nature's destructive forces while **Algar do Carvão** mesmerizes with its grandeur. The **Furnas** hot springs are equally compelling. Pristine biosphere reserves shield flora and fauna, including the rare **Azores bullfinch**. Offshore waters harbour a variety of sea life, where some of the best **whale and dolphin watching** in the world can be enjoyed.

There's a richness of culture, from the UNESCO-listed **Angra do Heroísmo** and **Pico Island vineyards** to the **Festas do Espírito Santo** and many other festivals. The Azores are also wonderfully outdoorsy. **Walking** and **hiking** trails crisscross every island. Watersports choices include **sailing**, **kayaking** and plenty of outstanding **dive sites**.

Whether you're visiting for a weekend or a week, our Top 10 guide brings together the best of everything this region has to offer, from the scenic village of **Vale das Furnas** to the magnificent **Capelinhos** volcano. The guide has useful tips throughout, from seeking out what's free to the best thermal springs, plus six easy-to-follow itineraries, designed to tie together a clutch of sights in a short space of time. Add inspiring photography and detailed maps, and you've got the essential pocket-sized travel companion. **Enjoy the book, and enjoy the Azores**.

Clockwise from top: **Angra do Heroísmo marina, Igreja de Santa Cruz in Praia da Vitória**, statue of Christ in Horta's **Igreja de São Salvador**, the picturesque **Caldeira das Sete Cidades**, Risso's dolphins, windmills at **Ponta da Espalamaca**, pink azalea at **Lagoa das Furnas**

Exploring the Azores

From UNESCO-listed vineyards and crater lakes to world-class whale watching and hot springs, the Azores are rich in natural beauty. Here are some ideas to make the most of your time in the archipelago. A two-day jaunt on São Miguel is enough time to explore all the "must-sees". Stay for a week and indulge in an exciting island-hop – the "triangle" that is Pico, Faial and São Jorge.

Pico's vineyards are protected by UNESCO as a World Heritage Site.

Horta marina on Faial is the primary port of call for transatlantic yachts.

Two Days on São Miguel

Day ❶
MORNING

Enjoy coffee and homemade pastries at **Louvre Michaelense** (see p59) in **Ponta Delgada** (see pp12–13). Later, explore Gruta do Carvão.

AFTERNOON

Marvel at the incredible **Caldeira das Sete Cidades** (see pp14–15), where the views from Miradouro da Vista do Rei are outstanding. Stop for coffee and cake in the village, then go **kayaking** (see p50) on the lakes.

Day ❷
MORNING

Have breakfast at **Mascote** (see p74), then head to **Cerâmica Vieira** (see p71) to see traditional pottery. Continue to **Vila Franca do Campo** (see p70).

AFTERNOON

Scenic **Vale das Furnas** (see pp18–19) deserves an entire afternoon, but lunch first at **Tony's** (see p75).

A Seven-Day Island-Hop: Faial, Pico and São Jorge

Day ❶

Spend the day in **Horta** (see pp26–7), starting with the Museu da Horta. Admire the murals at **Marina da Horta** (see p26) and have lunch at **Peter Café Sport** (see p96). Afterwards, browse the insightful exhibitions at **Casa dos Dabney** (see p26). End the day with dinner at the popular **Genuíno** (see p56).

Day ❷

Join a pre-booked excursion with **OceanEye** (see p94) and see Azorean marine life up-close. Later, enjoy seafood in the restaurants located at the marina. Visit **Capelinhos** volcano (see pp28–9) and see the impressive subterranean Centro de Interpreteção do Vulcão dos Capelinhos. Shop for souvenirs at **Centro de Artesanato do Capelo** (see p94) on the way back.

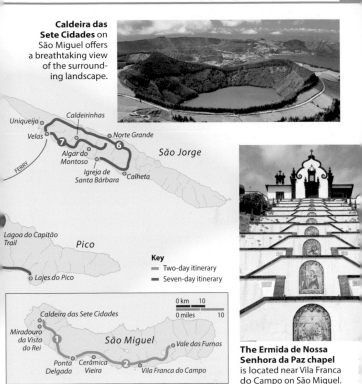

Caldeira das Sete Cidades on São Miguel offers a breathtaking view of the surrounding landscape.

Key
— Two-day itinerary
— Seven-day itinerary

The Ermida de Nossa Senhora da Paz chapel is located near Vila Franca do Campo on São Miguel.

Day ❸

Take a ferry across the channel to **Pico** (see pp88–91) and **Madalena** (see p93), your base for the next three days. Walk along the **Vinhas da Criação Velha Trail** (see p33). Pass by UNESCO-listed vineyards, then visit the windmill. Return in time for supper at **Ancoradouro** (see p57).

Day ❹

Head to **Lajes do Pico** (see p93) for a pre-booked **whale-watching** trip (see pp16–17). After lunch at **Pastelaria Aromas & Sabores** (see p96), visit the engrossing **Museu dos Baleeiros** (see p41). Finish the day over a glass of wine at **Cella Bar** (see p97).

Day ❺

Begin with the **Museu do Vinho** (see p32). Then, join a pre-booked guided tour at the **Centro de Interpretação da Paisagem da Cultura da Vinha da Ilha do Pico** (see p33). Hike the **Lagoa do Capitão Trail** (see p93) under **Montanha do Pico** (see p42).

Day ❻

Catch the ferry to **São Jorge** (see pp88–91) and explore **Velas** (see p92). Take a guided tour of the **Uniqueijo** cheese factory (see p92), then head to Norte Grande and lunch at **Amilcar** (see p97). Cross the island to **Calheta** (see p92) before skirting the coast to **Igreja de Santa Bárbara** (see p38).

Day ❼

Pack a picnic and take a taxi drop to the **Caldeirinhas–Norte Grande** walk (see p46); confirm the pick-up for afterwards. Later in the day, explore **Algar do Montoso** (see p92) on a pre-booked caving expedition. Finish with dinner at **Café Açor** (see p96).

These itineraries focus on four of the nine Azorean islands

Top 10 Azores Highlights

The striking volcanic landscape
of Capelinhos on the Faial coast

Azores Highlights	10	Diving Spots	24
Ponta Delgada	12	Horta	26
Caldeira das Sete Cidades	14	Capelinhos	28
Whale and Dolphin Watching	16	Algar do Carvão	30
Vale das Furnas	18	Paisagem da Cultura da Vinha da Ilha do Pico	32
Angra do Heroísmo	20		

🔟 Azores Highlights

A tranquil mid-Atlantic setting, dramatic volcanic scenery and splendid eco diversity make the Azores a compelling choice for outdoor enthusiasts and adventurous travellers. Each of the nine islands has its own distinctive character, and these standout attractions show why this remote Portuguese outpost has become one of the world's most desirable tourist destinations.

Ponta Delgada ①

The largest town in the Azores, Ponta Delgada is São Miguel's vibrant, ocean-facing hub and an ideal introduction to the archipelago (see pp12–13).

② Caldeira das Sete Cidades

This enormous volcanic crater hugs two idyllic lakes, and the views from its rim are awe-inspiring (see pp14–15).

Nort
Grane
Velas •
Capelinhos   Manadas •
⑧   *Faial*   Calheta
Horta   Paisagem da Cultura
⑦   ⑩ da Vinha da Ilha do Pico
Madalena   • São Roque do Pico
Candelária   *Pico*
São Mateus   Pi
Lajes do Pico •

Whale and Dolphin Watching ③

The Azores are one of the world's top whale- and dolphin-watching hot spots, with some 28 cetacean species seen here (see pp16–17).

⑤ Angra do Heroísmo

UNESCO has declared Angra a World Heritage Site, such is the splendour of its Renaissance buildings (see pp20–21).

④ Vale das Furnas

This is the archipelago's geothermal crowd-pleaser, with hot springs and fumaroles (see pp18–19).

Diving Spots 6

Luminous blue waters and glittering shoals of Atlantic and tropical fish distinguish the region as one of the richest marine habitats on the planet (see pp24–5).

7 Horta

A mid-ocean haven for yachts, Faial's port town has the world's largest collection of maritime paintings – all of them daubed on the marina walls and pier (see pp26–7).

Capelinhos 8

The destructive forces of nature are apparent here, the scene of a series of volcanic eruptions and seismic tremors in the late 1950s (see pp28–9).

Algar do Carvão 9

A dramatic, 2,000-year-old volcanic blast-hole, this dank, half-lit lava tube widens into a huge subterranean cavern (see pp30–31).

10 Paisagem da Cultura da Vinha da Ilha do Pico

Pico's landscape of volcanic vineyards and the island's centuries-old winemaking tradition are unique, a fact recognized by UNESCO (see pp32–3).

Most of these highlights are concentrated on and around four of the nine Azorean islands

🔟 ⭐ Ponta Delgada

The largest town in the Azores, historic Ponta Delgada melds maritime tradition with plenty of cultural clout. Set against a wide, sweeping bay, its impressive black-and-white chapels, churches, monasteries and museums overlook parks and gardens flecked with colour. Centuries of trade between Europe and the Americas placed the port at the vanguard of transatlantic commerce. Today, ocean-going cruise ships line the quay, flying the flags of far-flung nations. Take time to explore this capital and revel in its unhurried lifestyle.

1 Jardim e Palácio de Sant'Ana

This serene botanical garden **(above)** is admired for its flowering shrubs. Notable trees include the Norfolk Island pine and *pohutukawa*.

2 Arruda Açores Pineapple Plantation

Pineapple is a delicacy in the Azores. A tour of the estate takes in the greenhouses, and fruit can be purchased.

3 Igreja Matriz de São Sebastião

Richly sculptured motifs adorn the façade of this 16th-century church. The interior features cedar-wood carvings and hand-glazed *azulejos* (tiles).

4 Gruta do Carvão

Hidden under the town's western outskirts is the island's largest cave system. It is around 1,650 m (5,413 ft) long, and a part of it is open to the public.

5 Portas da Cidade

Built of regional stone in 1783, the city gates were originally set against the old harbour wall. Illustrious visitors, including members of the Portuguese royal family, would have passed under the graceful arches of this symbolic entrance **(below)**.

THE AZORES PINEAPPLE

Served in restaurants as a tropical fruit dessert, or combined with grilled spicy sausage for a tasty appetizer, pineapple is ubiquitous throughout the Azores. Brought to the islands from South America in the mid-19th century, pineapple was mainly cultivated in São Miguel, with greenhouse estates at Fajã de Baixo, near Ponta Delgada, and Vila Franco do Campo.

7 Portas do Mar

A maritime terminal for cruise ships and inter-island ferries **(left)**, the multifunctional "Sea Gates" complex also includes a top-notch marina. The quay is lined with shops, cafés and restaurants.

Map of Ponta Delgada

8 Forte de São Brás

This 16th-century fort is a fine example of military architecture. Today, it houses the Museu Militar dos Açores *(see p70)*.

9 Museu Carlos Machado

This museum *(see p41)*, opened in 1880, houses a collection of sacred art. It has an ethnography and natural history wing, too.

10 Igreja do Colégio

The expulsion of the Jesuits in 1760 left the altar of this church *(see p38)* only partially gilded. What was done, however, is still magnificent.

6 Convento e Santuário de Nossa Senhora da Esperança

The Convent of Our Lady of Hope *(see p39)* is a sanctuary for a revered piece of sacred art, Ecce Homo **(above)**, embellished with gems and metals.

NEED TO KNOW

Jardim e Palácio de Sant'Ana: **MAP U1**; Rua José Jácome Correia; (296) 301 000; garden: open 10am–5pm Tue–Sun; palace: open by appt only; adm €2 (garden), under 14s free, over 65s €1

Arruda Açores Pineapple Plantation: **MAP B6**; Rua Dr Augusto Arruda, Fajã de Baixo; (296) 384 438; open Apr–Sep: 9am–8pm; Oct–Mar: 9am–6pm

Gruta do Carvão: **MAP B6**; Rua do Paim; (296) 284 155; guided tours: 10:30am, 11:30am, 2:30pm, 3:30pm & 4:30pm daily; adm €7.50, under 15s €2, over 65s €3.50, under 7s free; www.grutadocarvao.pt

Convento e Santuário de Nossa Senhora da Esperança: **MAP U2**; Avenida Robertolvens 10; (296) 286 562; open 5:30–6:30pm daily

Forte de São Brás: **MAP U2**; Avenida Infante Dom Henrique; (296) 304 920; open 10am–6pm Mon–Fri; adm €3, under 18s & over 65s €1, under 12s free

Igreja do Colégio: **MAP U1**; Largo do Colégio; (296) 202 930; open 9am–12:30pm & 2–5:30pm Mon–Fri, 2–5:30pm Sat & Sun

■ The Largarta tourist train follows three themed audio city-tour routes: Historical, Beach and Gardens *(adm €8)*.

TOP 10 ⭐ Caldeira das Sete Cidades

One of the defining natural wonders of the Azores, the volcanic crater of Sete Cidades emerges from São Miguel's northwestern shoulder to dominate the island. With a 12-km (7-mile) circumference, it cups two enchanting lakes, one blue, one green. Sunk into the surrounding landscape is a collection of smaller lakes, droplets compared to their neighbours. A small village sits by the water's edge, a community dwarfed by its location but steeped in tradition – a place where romantic myth prevails. Take a day out and hike the green walls around this special place. The justifiably famous views will leave you speechless.

THE BIRTH OF "SABRINA"

In 1811, earth tremors shook the coast of São Miguel near Ponta do Escalvaldo, culminating in a submarine volcanic eruption. Four days later, in early June, a new island emerged – a circular cone 2 km (1 mile) in diameter and 100 m (328 ft) tall. Alerted by the explosions, the British sloop *Sabrina* set sail to investigate. The commanding officer planted a Union Jack on the landmass, claiming it for Great Britain and naming it Sabrina. But four months later the island sank, along with Britain's claim on it.

1 **Miradouro da Vista do Rei**
Named after the 1901 visit of King Dom Carlos, who stood at this overlook to admire the scenery, the viewpoint still affords a regal panorama **(above)**.

2 **Loja do Parque da Lagoa das Sete Cidades**
The park's shop and visitor centre stocks information about the area's walking trails, its flora and fauna, geology and classified heritage.

3 **Lagoa Azul**
The larger of the two lakes, the "Blue Lake" has a scattering of well-maintained bungalows and low-key watersports operations along its shores, where visitors can hire kayaks and stand-up paddleboards.

4 **Lagoa Verde**
The "Green Lake" **(below)** is so named because this side of the crater reflects the sunlight in shades of myrtle, jade and shamrock. To the northwest of the lake is a recreation zone.

Map of Caldeira das Sete Cidades

5 Mosteiros–Ponta do Escalvado–Ginetes–Rabo do Asno Trail

Nearly 12 km (7 miles) in length, this energizing coastal hike skirts the lower outside walls of the caldera and takes in the Ponta do Escalvado **(above)**.

10 Sete Cidades Village

Nestling at Lagoa Azul's edge is the idyllic village of Sete Cidades. Distinguished by its Neo-Gothic church **(below)**, the secluded hamlet appears cradled by the enormous crater.

6 Mosteiros

Appreciated for its black-sand beach and natural rock pools, this coastal village has some excellent seafood restaurants *(see p75)*.

9 Lagoa do Canário

In spring butterflies can be seen flitting over azaleas as hikers follow the Mata do Canário foot-path to the water's edge.

7 Miradouro da Boca do Inferno

The "Hell's Mouth" look-out presents the Santiago, Rasa and Azul lakes in one of the Azores' finest natural canvases.

8 Vista do Rei–Sete Cidades Trail

The trail for this pleasant ramble begins at the Vista do Rei viewpoint and snakes around the top of Lagoa Verde.

NEED TO KNOW

MAP A5

Loja do Parque da Lagoa das Sete Cidades: Module No. 5, Lagoa Azul, Sete Cidades; (296) 249 016; open 9am–12:30pm & 1:30–5pm daily; closed Oct–Apr: Sat & Sun

■ A pioneer of social and inclusive tourism in the Azores, Cresaçor *(Loja Eco-Atlântida, Rua Nova 45; (296) 098 866)* provides amenities to those with limited mobility or who have learning difficulties. It has an eco-store in Sete Cidades where visitors can rent kayaks, paddle-boards and mountain bikes. The company also organizes walking tours and jeep safaris.

■ Restaurante São Nicolau is one of the few dining options in Sete Cidades and is convenient for a light meal *(Rua da Igreja 18A; (916) 138 002)*.

TOP 10 ⭐ Whale and Dolphin Watching

Moored between two continents and surrounded by the Atlantic Ocean, the Azores archipelago is one of the world's premier whale- and dolphin-watching destinations. Attracted by the mild, nutrient-rich currents of the Gulf Stream, some 28 species of cetaceans have been sighted here. The majority of these marine mammals arrive early in the year for the warm summer season, escorted by pods of intelligent, lively dolphins. Take an excursion out to sea and admire these creatures in their natural habitat.

WHALE PURSUITS

American whalers, who arrived around 1765, introduced whaling to the Azores. Over the next two centuries, numerous whaling companies were set up. The *cachalote* (sperm whale) was taken frequently, the carcass beached and the blubber melted down for oil. Later the entire animal was used. The mid-20th century saw global whale numbers fall alarmingly and by 1987 whaling had ended in the Azores.

2 Risso's Dolphin
Distinguished by their rounded head and curiously scarred frame, resident populations of Risso's are usually found in deeper water. They can be extremely frisky.

3 Common Bottlenose Dolphin
Seen all year, these sociable and inquisitive animals never fail to please. Their frolicking and high-flying antics elicit applause and smiles as wide as theirs.

4 Blue Whale
This is the largest animal (above) ever known to have lived on the Earth. Visitors are most likely to see these sleek, agile swimmers off Pico's southern coast, from around March to the beginning of June.

1 Atlantic Spotted Dolphin
Cruising into Azorean waters with their calves around June and staying until the end of November, these dolphins (below) gather in their hundreds.

WWW.ESPACOTALASSA.COM   TOMAS H-106-AL

⑤ Striped Dolphin

Named for the long, striped outline running on either side of the body, this species is found fairly regularly during the summer, autumn and early winter.

⑥ Sei Whale

Another ocean-going giant and one of the fastest, reaching speeds over 50 kmph (30 mph). Spring is the best time to see them.

⑦ Fin Whale

Measuring up to 27 m (90 ft), this is the world's second-biggest whale. Slender and solitary, it can be spotted from March to September.

⑧ Short-Beaked Common Dolphin

This species (right) is identified by a distinctive "hourglass" pattern on their flanks. They often gather in groups to bow ride in front of boats.

⑨ Sperm Whale

Iconic to the Azores, this is the archipelago's most commonly sighted whale **(above)**. Summer months are particularly rewarding, with groups often appearing near the coast off São Miguel, Terceira, Faial and Pico.

⑩ Short-Finned Pilot Whale

Recognized by its bulbous melon head and dorsal fin located far forward on the body, this whale is in fact a larger member of the dolphin group. They are usually spotted from mid-May to October.

NEED TO KNOW

Espaço Talassa: **MAP N3**; (292) 672 010; www. espacotalassa.com

Futurismo: **MAP V2**; (296) 628 522; www. futurismo.pt

Museu dos Baleeiros: **MAP N3**; Rua dos Baleeiros 13, Lajes do Pico, Pico; (292) 679 340; open Apr–Sep: 10am–5:30pm Tue–Sun, Oct–Mar: 9:30am–5pm Tue–Sun; adm €2 (free Sun), under 25s €1, under 14s free

Museu de Cachalotes e Lulas: **MAP L2**; Avenida Machado Serpa, Madalena, Pico; (292) 623 345; open 10am–5:30pm Tue–Fri, 1:30–5pm Sat & Sun; adm

■ The former spotting stations, or *vigias*, now make great land-based whale watching posts.

■ Stay up to date about the world of whales at www.whalewatching azores.com/blog.

🔟 ⭐ Vale das Furnas

Draped over a volcanic depression, the Furnas Valley is a vivid landscape moulded within the rim of a colossal caldera. A scenic village and a splendid lake sit on a beautiful valley floor painted every shade of green. Simmering beneath this picturesque veneer, however, is a rumbling underworld of steam and boiling water – the *caldeiras*. Spluttering to the surface, these bubbling and burping hot springs are São Miguel's geothermal crowd-pleasers.

Caldeiras das Furnas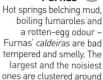

Hot springs belching mud, boiling fumaroles and a rotten-egg odour – Furnas' *caldeiras* are bad tempered and smelly. The largest and the noisiest ones are clustered around the town centre **(right)**.

2 Parque Terra Nostra

A botanist's paradise, this historic park has more than 600 varieties of camellias, a collection of rare cycads and pretty amaryllis. Take a stroll on the Avenue of Palms and then a dip in the geothermal pool *(see p45)*.

3 Ermida de Nossa Senhora das Vitórias

On Lake Furnas' southern shore is this Neo-Gothic funerary chapel **(below)**, the final resting place of botanist José do Canto (1820–1898) and his wife Maria. The building itself is closed, but visit the nearby gardens.

NEED TO KNOW

Parque Terra Nostra: **MAP E5**; Largo Marquês da Praia; (296) 549 090; open 10:30am–4:30pm daily; adm €10, under 11s €5, under 2s free; www. parqueterranostra.com

Observatório Microbiano dos Açores: **MAP E5**; Antigo Chalé de Misturas, Caldeiras; (296) 584 765 (call ahead for guided tours and mineral-water tastings); open 10am–5pm Tue–Fri, 2:30–6pm Sun (closed Mon, Sep–Jun; Sat); adm €1.50, under 18s 75¢, over 65s €1, under 3s free

Poça da Dona Beija: **MAP E5**; Lomba das Barracas; (296) 584 256;

open 8:30am–11pm daily (last adm 10:15pm); adm €8, under 7s €6; www. pocadadonabeija.com

Centro de Monitorização e Investigação das Furnas: **MAP E6**; Rua Lagoa das Furnas; (296) 584 436; open May–Sep: 9am–6pm daily; Oct–Apr: 9am–5pm Tue–Sat; adm €3, over 65s & under 15s €1.50, under 7s free

■ Tony's is renowned for its hospitality and *cozido das Furnas (see p75)*.

■ Look for the snack kiosk in the car park selling *milho cozido* (corn on the cob), boiled in sacks suspended in the *caldeiras'* waters.

5 Poça da Dona Beija

This hot springs complex **(left)** allows visitors to soak in five open-air rock pools fed by a mineral-rich thermal spring. At night the spa is illumined with spotlights, lending it a romantic appeal.

6 Centro de Monitorização e Investigação das Furnas

This research centre highlights the lake's eco-system and local flora and fauna. Look for the "volcanic bomb", a rare sample of pyroclastic debris from the 1439 Pico do Gaspar eruption.

7 Miradouro do Pico do Ferro

A bird in flight couldn't get a better view of the Furnas Valley. The panorama embraces the lake and the town, which resembles a Lilliputian hamlet from this height.

4 Observatório Microbiano dos Açores

Visitors can find answers to anything they might want to know about the microbial diversity at the educative Microbe Observatory of the Azores.

MINERAL WEALTH

In 1930 eminent Azorean hydrologist Armando da Cunha Narciso (1890–1948) declared Furnas Valley the most exuberant and abundant region of thermal waters in Europe. An incredible 20 different mineral waters gush from the ground in the village. Water from the Água do Padre José fountain, for example, is traditionally used to make thermal teas. However, due to its chemical structure this water causes green tea to turn purple. Coffee anyone?

---

8 Lagoa das Furnas

The second-largest lake **(below)** on São Miguel *(see p42)* has a variety of wildfowl, which includes ring-necked ducks and greater scaups. Hiking the 11-km (7-mile) nature trail around the lake is a great way to spend three hours.

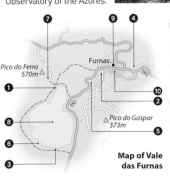

9 Furnas Village

Sitting in the lap of the valley, Furnas is one of São Miguel's most frequently visited spots. The village's claim to fame is its volcanic heritage, lush gardens and unique gastronomy.

10 Cozido das Furnas

Chicken, beef, pork, spicy *chouriço* sausage, black pudding, yam, sweet potato, carrot, cabbage and kale are cooked below ground for six hours to make the most succulent one-pot dish travellers are likely to taste *(see p55)*.

Map of Vale das Furnas

Pico do Ferro 570m

Furnas

Pico do Gaspar 373m

🔟 ⭐ Angra do Heroísmo

A UNESCO World Heritage Site, Angra do Heroísmo's Renaissance old town, scenic bay and pretty gardens make it one of the Azores' most beautiful places. From the 1600s to the mid-19th century, Angra was a port of strategic importance. The age of sail and Portuguese discoveries brought with it wealth and prestige – a prosperity invested in palaces, monasteries and churches. Visitors will enjoy the town's fascinating history and the architecture that defines it.

① Santíssimo Salvador da Sé

This cathedral is noted for the altar's 18th-century antependium, a superb example of Terceiran tracery. Also look for the lectern crafted from Brazilian jacaranda and inlaid with whale ivory.

③ Museu de Angra do Heroísmo

The diverse collection **(left)** at this museum (see p40) delves into regional history and the Azores' relations with the world. Pieces such as the exquisite 16th-century planetary astrolabe are truly stunning.

② Rua Direita

The town's most attractive thoroughfare has elegant buildings with colour-trimmed windows and filigree wrought-iron balconies. It takes visitors from the harbour to Praça Velha, the central square.

④ Igreja da Misericórdia

The blue façade of this 18th-century church (see p38) defines Angra's harbour. It stands on the site of the first hospital built in the Azores.

⑤ Palácio dos Capitães Generais

The 18th-century Palace of the Captain Generals is complemented by the adjoining Igreja do Santo Inácio de Loyola, which houses one of the best collections of 17th-century Dutch tiles outside the Netherlands **(below)**.

⑥ Palácio Bettencourt

Noted for its handsome portico, this early-18th-century palace is now a public library. Its archive has a valuable collection of rare books. This literary treasure can be viewed by appointment.

⑦ Convento de São Gonçalo

Angra's largest and oldest convent (see p39) is a feast of Baroque and Rococo architecture. The altar is flanked by *azulejos* (tiles) dating from the 18th century.

JOÃO VAZ CORTE-REAL

João Vaz Corte-Real (1420–96) is credited with the European discovery of Newfoundland in 1473 – a landmass that he called "New Land of the Codfish". Appointed Angra's Capitão Donatário in 1474, he was a founding member of the society that supported the construction of the first hospital in the Azores, built in 1492 on a site now occupied by the Igreja da Misericórdia.

Fortaleza de São João Baptista ⑧

Created by Filipe II during Spain's annexation of Portugal *(see p36)*, Angra's castle **(right)** houses the first church built after the restoration of the Portuguese monarchy.

Angra do Heroísmo with Monte Brasil in the background

Map of Angra do Heroísmo

⑨ Outeiro da Memória

The much-reproduced rooftop view of the town, its bay and Monte Brasil beyond is taken near this obelisk. Erected in 1846 in memory of King Dom Pedro IV, it stands on the site of the first fort built in the Azores in 1474.

⑩ Jardim Duque da Terceira

Teeming with roses, magnolias, cycads and tree ferns, this garden is an urban oasis. The grounds were originally part of the Convento de São Francisco.

NEED TO KNOW

Santíssimo Salvador da Sá: **MAP U4**; Rua da Sé; (295) 217 850; open 8am–5:30pm Mon–Fri, 9:30am–6:30pm Sat, 9am–noon & 5–7pm Sun

Museu de Angra do Heroísmo: **MAP V3**; Ladeira de São Francisco; (295) 240 800; open Apr–Sep: 10am–5:30pm

Tue–Sun; Oct–Mar: 9:30am–5pm Tue–Sun; adm €2 (free Sun), over 65s & under 26s €1, under 15s free

Palácio dos Capitães Generais: **MAP U3**; Rua do Palácio; (295) 402 300; open 10am–5pm Tue–Sun; adm €3, under 15s free

Palácio Bettencourt: **MAP U4**; Rua da Rosa; (295) 401 000; open 9am–5pm Mon–Fri

Fortaleza de São João Baptista: **MAP M6**; Monte Brasil; (295) 214 011; open 10–11am & 2–6pm daily

Jardim Duque da Terceira: **MAP V3**; open summer: 8am–midnight daily; winter: 8am–10pm daily

■ A guided cultural walking tour is organized by Angra 2000 *(angra2000.com)*.

Following pages Scenic landscape of Faial dotted with hydrangeas and windmills

TOP 10 ⭐ Diving Spots

With their rich marine biodiversity, the Azores offer some of the best diving conditions in the world. High visibility in temperate, crystalline waters and a seafloor sculpted from lava exemplify this vast maritime region. There are nearly 100 diving sites found across the archipelago, each one a veritable underwater wonderland teeming with sea life. The impressive subaquatic landscape features shipwrecks, volcanic seamounts, and warrens of basaltic caves and tunnels. In places, marine reserves and archaeological parks have been established to showcase fragile reefs and the Azores' seafaring heritage. Visitors who dive off the nine islands will have the opportunity to swim with some of nature's greatest marine life.

1 Dori

The wreck of the *Edwin L Drake*, a former Liberty ship **(below)** that was built in the US during World War II and sank off the southern coast of São Miguel in 1964, is a designated subaquatic archaeological park. Much of the stern is still intact. Marine life is abundant on this artificial reef.

2 Ilhéus das Formigas

This outcrop of scattered rock **(above)** 33 nautical miles (61 km) southeast of São Miguel is noted for its rich variety of pelagic fishes. Wait for favourable sea conditions to explore this marine reserve.

3 Gruta dos Enxaréus

The mysterious pirate cave hidden at the foot of cliffs near Santa Cruz on Flores reveals a submerged cavern *(see p99)*, the dark corridors of which are patrolled by beady-eyed stingrays.

4 Caneiro dos Meros

This dive spot is well known for having the greatest concentration of dusky grouper in the Azores. These fish glide through the archipelago's first and only voluntary marine reserve, in front of Vila do Corvo, Corvo's tiny harbour.

5 Ilhéu do Topo

A protected reserve for birds, Ilhéu do Topo (see p92) has a fertile ecosystem that extends underwater, where yellow-mouth barra-cuda mingle with barred hogfish **(left)**. The dive site is off the southeastern tip of São Jorge.

6 Gruta e Ilhéu Negro

The best way to enjoy this dive is to make it on a bright and cloudless day. The shards of sunlight beaming through the ice-blue sea will illuminate the entrance to the submerged cave, which is burrowed under Faial's Monte da Guia **(below)**.

7 Naufrágio Terceirense

Exploring the wreck of the *Terceirense* that sank in 1968 outside the port of Praia on Graciosa is rewarded with an array of colourful fish, including canary damsels, rainbow wrasses and parrotfish.

8 Banco Dom João de Castro

Grey triggerfish and Atlantic bonito are among the sea life found congregating in and around this intriguing submarine volcano, located 35 nautical miles (65 km) from Terceira.

RICH MARINE LIFE IN THE AZORES

The Azores are a marine life hot spot. Nearly 30 of the world's 80-odd cetaceans have been seen here, including humpbacks and minkes. Dolphins scythe the waves, and loggerhead turtles row through the water as manta rays and devil rays glide by. The mid-ocean seamounts attract both blue and whale sharks, and Portuguese man o' wars gather by the thousand. Texturing the seabed are purple sea stars, yellow encrusting anemones, fireworms and nudibranchs. Adding tropical brilliance are parrotfish and wrasses.

9 Banco Princesa Alice

It's worth making the 50-nautical-mile (93-km) voyage out of Madalena on Pico to reach this dive spot popular for pelagic species such as the Chilean devil ray **(below)** and Galapagos shark.

10 Banco Dollabarat

Sited 20 nautical miles (37 km) to the northeast of Santa Maria and 3 nautical miles (5 km) from the Ilhéus das Formigas, this reserve is frequented by manta rays and sharks.

NEED TO KNOW

Parque Arqueológico Subaquático da Baía de Angra do Heroísmo: **MAP M6**; Angra do Heroísmo, Terceira; (295) 240 800

■ Visit www.dive.visit azores.com for information about the islands' diving sites and centres.

■ The best time to dive in the Azores is from June to September.

■ Parque Arqueológico Subaquático da Baía de Angra do Heroísmo is an underwater archaeological park that features a number of shipwrecks and abandoned anchors.

ᵀᴼᴾ⑩ ⭐ Horta

Vibrant Horta on Faial is the yachting capital of the Azores, having served as an anchorage for caravels, clippers and seaplanes for hundreds of years. The late 19th century saw the installation of the first transatlantic cable stations, and today the town's cultural heritage draws on this link between the land and the sea. Museums bear testimony to the island's former whaling industry, while the mild climate helps parks and gardens flourish.

1 Casa dos Dabney

Out of Boston, the Dabney family settled on Faial in 1806. The cellar of their summer house *(see p40)* is now home to a poignant exhibition that chronicles three early generations of the family.

2 Casa-Museu Manuel de Arriaga

Manuel de Arriaga *(see p37)*, first president of the Republic of Portugal, was elected in 1911. His Horta home has been converted into a museum that celebrates the life of this political intellectual.

3 Jardim Botânico do Faial

Shrubs such as *Myrica faya* (after which Faial was named), Azores buckthorn and Azorean laurel are three of the endemic plants showcased in this public garden *(see p94)*.

4 Marina da Horta

Horta's popular marina **(above)** has berths for 300 yachts, and welcomes nearly 1,500 boats each year. Visiting crews leave their colourful calling cards on the harbour pier and walls – the largest maritime painting collection in the world.

5 Museu de Scrimshaw

The spear-like tusk of a narwhal, an Arctic whale dubbed the unicorn of the sea, is one of the more unusual exhibits **(left)** at this well-known museum *(see p40)*. The exhibition of scrimshaw *(see p60)* is among the most extensive anywhere.

6 Museu da Horta

A salon in this museum *(see p40)* is dedicated to the fig tree pith sculptures **(left)** of Faial-born Euclides da Silveira Rosa (1910–1979). The museum also displays other eclectic exhibits.

8 Fábrica da Baleia de Porto Pim

In its heyday this former factory was one of the most productive whaling stations in the Azores. An exhibition **(left)** and the engrossing interpretation centre tell its story.

Map of Horta

10 Miradouro do Monte da Guia

Sited near a chapel, this viewpoint is 100 m (328 ft) above sea level. The lofty views focus on Porto Pim and Horta, while Pico dominates the horizon.

9 Igreja de São Salvador

This 17th-century church (see p39) is known for its gilded woodwork and chapels (right). The altar of the Holy Sacrament is fronted by an engraved silver antependium.

7 Aquário de Porto Pim

Various fish species are cared for here *(see p90)* before being rehoused in aquariums abroad.

NEED TO KNOW

Casa dos Dabney: MAP T4; Complexo Monte da Guia; (292) 240 685; open 9am–12:30pm & 1:30–5pm; closed Oct–Apr: Sat & Sun

Casa-Museu Manuel de Arriaga: MAP S3; Travessa de São Francisco; (292) 293 361; open Apr–Sep: 10am–5:30pm Tue–Sun; Oct–Mar: 9:30am–5pm Tue–Sun; adm €2 (free Sun), under 14s free

Jardim Botânico do Faial: MAP J3; Rua da São Lourenço 23; (292) 207 360;

open 9am–6pm daily (Oct–Apr: to 5pm Tue–Sat); adm €7.50, under 15s & over 65s €3.75, under 7s free

Museu de Scrimshaw: MAP T3; Rua José Azevedo 9; closed Sun; adm €2.50, under 12s free; www.petercafesport.com

Museu da Horta & Igreja de São Salvador: MAP T2; Largo Duque d'Avila e Bolama; (292) 392 784; open Apr–Sep: 10am–5:30pm Tue–Sun; Oct–Mar: 9:30am–5pm Tue–Sun; adm €2 (free Sun), under 14s free

Aquário de Porto Pim: MAP S4; (964) 971 484; open Jun–Sep: 10am–5pm Tue–Sun; Oct–May: 10am–5pm Tue–Fri, 2–5:30pm Sat; adm €4, under 12s free

Fábrica da Baleia de Porto Pim: MAP T4; Monte da Guia; (292) 292 140; open 10am–6pm Mon–Fri (Nov–Mar: to 5pm); adm €5, under 16s & over 65s €2, under 7s free

■ Dive with whale sharks at the Princesa Alice seamount *(see p25)*. Visit www.norbertodiver.pt for more details.

TOP 10 ⭐ Capelinhos

Thunderous earthquakes, volcanic eruptions, molten lava lakes and a cloud of muddy debris – the explosive episodes of 1957–8 defined an era and forever altered the social and geological fabric of Capelinhos, located in western Faial. But from the ashes rose one of the most coveted geosites in the Azores. Travellers should start below ground at the futuristic visitor centre before exploring this lunar-like landscape by heading to the top of the lighthouse, then traversing the volcano trail, crunching basalt underfoot along the way.

1 Capelinhos Volcano

Located in the far west of Faial, this is one of the Azores' greatest attractions **(above)**. Earthquakes and submarine eruptions in 1957–8 added an area of around 2.5 sq km (1 sq mile) to the landmass (see p42).

THE CAPELINHOS ERUPTION

The tremors that began on 16 September 1957 heralded a continuous period of volcanic and seismic activity around Capelinhos. The boiling sea and hissing vapour developed into violent explosions. By mid-March 1958, a new island was attached to the mainland by a cord of steaming black ash. The Capelinhos eruption was a seminal event that destroyed 300 houses and made 2,000 people homeless.

2 Formação do Arquipélago dos Açores

The thousands of years it took to form the present-day Azores is condensed into an engaging 3D film shown at the Capelinhos interpretative centre. It houses an exhibition hall that displays a sample of volcanic rock collected from each island.

3 Sala Holograma

Inside the interpretative centre is the Hologram Hall where holographic animation re-creates the 13 months of submarine and subaerial tremors and eruptions before the final seismic blast.

4 Farol da Punta dos Capelinhos

The highlight for many is the climb to the top of the now-abandoned lighthouse **(below)**, the only building that withstood the eruptions.

5 Parque Florestal do Capelo

The Capelo Recreational Forest Reserve *(see p94)* offers a leafy alternative to the stark, barren Capelinhos environment. A protected area, the park is noted for its endemic flora, in particular an abundance of laurel.

6 Ten Volcanoes Trail

The ascent from the interpretative centre leads hikers through the fertile lowlands of Capelo before climbing towards Faial's immense *caldeira*, following an alignment of some of the island's oldest volcanic cones along the way *(see p47)*.

7 Protected Landscape

The unique lunar-like landscape created in the wake of the eruption, considered one of the most definitive volcanic events of the 20th century, is classified as a protected nature reserve of geological, biological and aesthetic interest.

8 Centro de Interpretação do Vulcão dos Capelinhos

This underground interpretative centre **(above)** provides plenty of information about the Capelinhos eruption and volcanology *(see p91)*.

9 Capelo– Capelinhos Trail

A walk of moderate difficulty, the trail begins at the Cabeço Verde volcanic cone in the Capelo Recreational Forest Reserve. The 55-m (180-ft) deep Furna Ruim lava cave en route is a photographic highlight.

10 Caldeira

Encircled by an emerald mantle of native vegetation splashed with lilac-hued hydrangeas, the island's crater **(below)** offers a broad, inspirational prospect over the Capelinhos peninsula *(see p91)*.

NEED TO KNOW

Centro de Interpretação do Vulcão dos Capelinhos: **MAP G2**; Capelinhos; (292) 200 470; open May–Sep: 9am–6pm daily; Oct–Apr: 9am–5pm Tue–Sat (call ahead for guided tours); adm €10, 7–14s & over 65s €5, under 7s free; www. parquesnaturais.azores. gov.pt

■ There is a café-bar in the foyer of the interpretative centre.

■ The Cabeço do Canto is a good hike if you're looking for a shorter alternative to the Capelo-Capelinhos Trail. It is a steep 20-minute walk to the lookout point, where you can enjoy fine views over Capelinhos.

■ Visitors can also explore Casa dos Botes *(Porto do Comprido; open Jun–Sep: 10am–1pm & 2–6pm daily)* in Capelinhos, a former whalers' boathouse recovered from the ashes of the volcanic eruption and subsequently rebuilt. It serves as a reminder of Faial's once flourishing whaling industry.

TOP 10 ⭐ Algar do Carvão

Set in the heart of Terceira, the Algar do Carvão cave system is a compelling subterranean spectacle. Formed two millennia ago during the dying days of a fiery volcano, this huge lava tube appears as though blasted from the island's core, its walls and ceiling bearing the scars of a fierce meltdown. Entering this underworld of stalactites and stalagmites is to tread the dark recesses of the earth, where nature is the architect of some extraordinary chambers and caverns. Deeper still, a pit cradles a lake. Linger in this ethereal hollow and reflect on the powerful forces that created it.

1 Bola Gasosa

A striking geological anomaly greeting visitors as they enter the first chamber is the "gaseous ball" – the walled imprint of a huge basaltic gas bubble **(right)**. Its shape resembles the wide-open eye of a giant.

3 Caldeira Guilherme Moniz

Algar do Carvão is located near Terceira's central crater, the 15-km (9-mile) perimeter of which places it among the largest in the Azores. The region falls within the boundaries of a natural reserve, an area of Macaronesian scrubland and peat bogs **(left)**.

4 Lagoa

Set 80 m (262 ft) within the belly of the cave is a lake. Nourished by rainfall, this hidden lagoon is normally around 15 m (50 ft) deep but dries up almost completely in summer due to low precipitation.

5 Stalactites

The world's largest concentration of amorphous silica stalactites **(below)** is found here. Up to 1 m (3 ft) long, these rare milky-white structures ornament large areas of the ceiling.

2 Boca do Algar do Carvão

The mouth of the cave bristles with endemic flora – a treat for botanists and speleologists. There are 34 species of liverwort and 22 varieties of moss.

NEED TO KNOW

MAP M5 ▪ Algar do Carvão ▪ (295) 212 992

Open Apr–May: 2:30–5pm daily; Jun–Sep: 2–6pm daily; Oct–Mar: 2:30–5pm Tue, Wed, Fri & Sat

Adm €8, under 12s free

▪ The Associação Os Montanheiros *(Rua da Rocha 8, Angra do Heroísmo; (295) 212 992; www.montanheiros.com)* is an association of speleologists that facilitates access to the vast network of caves spread across the archipelago *(see p80)*.

Visitors inside Algar do Carvão cave

7 Cave-Dwelling Spider

Sharp-eyed cavers might chance upon the elusive *Turinyphia cavernicola*, an endemic spider found only in Algar do Carvão. The webs of these cave-dwelling arachnids can be spotted between the ancient fissures.

8 Other Troglobitic Insects

Perfectly adapted to the underground life is *Trechus terceiranus*, a copper-coloured beetle endemic to Terceira. Another Algar resident that will interest entomologists is *Lithobius obscuras azorae*, a species of centipede.

9 The "Cathedral"

Of massive proportions, the cavern's inner chamber draws gasps for its imposing domed roof streaked with glassy obsidian. The vault's pure acoustics mean it is often the stage for subterranean music concerts.

10 Furnas do Enxofre

Sulphurous fumaroles **(below)** near the Algar cave complex bubble up from the tangled undergrowth over which a purpose-built footpath snakes and dips.

A 2,000-YEAR-OLD NATURAL WONDER

Algar do Carvão is a huge lava tube around 100 m (328 ft) in length, a cavern in a basaltic scoria cone formed during a volcanic eruption some 2,000 years ago. The outer chamber can be accessed via a vertical vent that drops 45 m (147 ft) from the mouth of the cave. A second conduit falls to an inner cave, the base of which is filled by a lake, situated 80 m (262 ft) from the uppermost reaches of the tube. The cave is classified as a Regional Natural Monument.

6 Ferns and Other Flora

The underside of the cave entrance is radiant enough to sustain ferns, their delicate emerald fronds often backlit by sunlight. Green algae and mould can be spotted in the cave's deeper recesses.

TOP 10 ⭐ Paisagem da Cultura da Vinha da Ilha do Pico

The UNESCO-protected "Landscape of Pico Island Vineyard Culture" is made up of coastal vineyards, corralled into pockets by basalt walls. Here, the island's winemaking tradition is evident in the distilleries, cellars and warehouses in hamlets where *adegas* (wineries) have been producing wine for centuries. Plan a visit during harvest, which is celebrated with song and dance, and when festivals pair the best wines with home-style food.

1 Museu do Vinho

A former Carmelite convent building houses the wine museum *(see p40)*. The grounds can be seen from a platform set over the *currais* (double walls) and *curraletas* (basalt-walled plots) that enclose the vines.

2 Rilheiras

Numerous lava slabs **(left)** have been moulded by *rilheiras* (wheel tracks) of carts laden with goods hauled by oxen, once the only effective method of transportation. Many are found near the coast.

3 Cooperativa Vitivinícola da Ilha do Pico

A guided visit to this wine cooperative *(see p93)* includes a tasting of the island's best-known wines. Prominent labels include Basalto and Terras de Lava.

NEED TO KNOW

Museu do Vinho: **MAP L2**; Rua do Carmo, near Madalena; (292) 679 348; open summer: 10am–5:30pm Tue–Sun, winter: 9:30am–5pm Tue–Sun; adm €2 (free Sun), 14–25-year-olds & over 65s €1, under 13s free

Azores Wine Company: **MAP L2**; Rua do Poço Velho, Cais do Mourato; (912) 530 237; call ahead to reserve a guided visit and wine tasting

Centro de Interpretação da Paisagem da Cultura da Vinha da Ilha do Pico: **MAP M2**; Rua do Lajido, Santa Luzia; (956) 896 313; open May–Sep: 9am–12:30pm & 1:30–6pm daily; Oct–Apr: 9am–12:30pm & 1:30–5pm Tue–Fri; book in advance for a guided tour of the vineyards

■ On most days, women in traditional costume can be found on the Moinho do Frade verandah selling local handicrafts.

4 Rola-Pipas

Scout the water's edge and spot the smooth telltale ramps that are hollowed out of serrated basalt. These facilitated the movement of wine barrels to the nearest port. They are called *rola-pipas*, and it was no easy task levelling out the stubborn terrain this way.

Pico's vineyards enclosed by basalt walls

9 Centro de Interpretação da Paisagem da Cultura da Vinha da Ilha do Pico

This interpretative centre **(above)** explains Pico's viniculture and highlights the wines produced here. A visit to a traditional distillery is included, and there's an opportunity to taste the wines.

VINES, VINEYARDS AND WINE

Popular lore suggests that the parish priest of Lajes was the first to plant vines on Pico in the late 15th century. The mid-1500s saw the advent of Pico's viniculture but stony, lava-strewn soil and salt-laced squalls made cultivation arduous. The solution was to build *currais* from the loose volcanic debris to shield the vines from winds and sea spray, and to retain the daytime heat. These plots or *curraletas* characterize Pico's vineyard landscape.

5 Santana–Lajido Trail

Beginning in Santana village, this trail takes visitors past the Baía do Gasparal and its former cargo dock. There are fine examples of *rola-pipas* here. The route skirts the coast to Lajido, a hamlet known for its fig-distilled firewater.

7 Vinhas da Criação Velha Trail

This walk offers stunning views of Pico and Faial and skirts the impressive vineyards to pass the harbour, ending at Porto do Calhau. Look out for the *Azorina vidalii (see p53)* with its lovely bell-shaped blooms **(left)**.

10 Moinho do Frade

The iconic cylindrical windmill with its red bonnet **(below)** looms over the noted Criação Velha vineyards that lie west of Madalena. Once used to mill grain, the carefully restored landmark offers a wonderful view across the vicinity.

6 Tidal Wells

These box-shaped wells were built to capture fresh water running underground to the sea, the accumulation of which was influenced by tidal currents.

8 Azores Wine Company

Drop by this stylish modern winery for tastings of Terrantez do Pico, a unique Azorean grape variety that almost became extinct.

The Top 10 of Everything

Capela do Santíssimo Sacramento Igreja Matriz de São Sebastião in Ponta Delagada, São Miguel

Moments in History	**36**
Churches and Chapels	**38**
Museums	**40**
Natural Wonders	**42**
Natural Swimming Pools and Thermal Springs	**44**
Walks and Hikes	**46**

Outdoor Activities	**50**
Birdlife	**52**
Traditional Azorean Cuisine	**54**
Restaurants	**56**
Places to Shop	**58**
Arts and Crafts	**60**
Traditional Festivals	**62**

🔟 Moments in History

1 Discovery

The first map to depict the Azores was the 1351 *Medici-Laurentian Atlas*, which outlined the seven islands of the Central and Eastern Groups. Recent evidence suggests the islands were first occupied, perhaps by Vikings, between 700 and 850. The first island spotted by Portuguese explorers, sometime between 1427 and 1432, was Santa Maria. Flores and Corvo, in the Western Group, were not discovered until 1452.

Medici-Laurentian Atlas

2 Settlement

By the mid-15th century Portuguese and Flemish explorers had visited the archipelago. Named *Açores* by early settlers after they supposedly sighted goshawks *(see p52)*, the first islands to be populated were Santa Maria and São Miguel, followed by Terceira and Graciosa in 1450. By 1466 settlements had appeared on São Jorge, Faial and Pico. Flores was colonized around 1504, while Corvo had the first semblance of a community by 1548.

3 Commercial Development

By the mid-16th century the islands provided anchorage for vessels returning from India. The colonization of Brazil by Portugal and the discovery of America also led to development of infrastructure across the Azores.

4 Spanish Invasion

In 1583, Spanish troops, led by Álvaro de Bazán, clashed with islanders and French and English soldiers on Terceira. The defence crumbled under the Spanish army. Terceira and the Kingdom of Portugal were taken over by Filipe II (1521–1598). In 1640 the Portuguese monarchy was restored and the Azores liberated.

5 Liberals and Absolutists

Portugal's 1820 Liberal revolution reverberated across the Azores. The Absolutists targeted Terceira, the last Liberal stronghold, and in 1829 attempted unsuccessfully to land at Vila da Praia. Following their defeat, it was renamed Praia da Vitória *(see p78)*. Angra became the capital of Portugal until 1833. It was later named Angra do Heroísmo.

A 16th-century painting depicting the Spanish invasion

6 World War II

The archipelago's strategic value increased after the US entered World War II. Lajes Field was built on Terceira in 1943, an air base from which Allied forces fought German U-boats. Today, Lajes remains a US-Portuguese military base, contributing towards NATO's strategic role.

A fighter jet at present-day Lajes Field

7 The Capelinhos Eruption

A series of earth tremors in September 1957 led to an under-water volcanic eruption off the Faial coast, near Capelinhos (see pp28–9). Explosions in 1958 formed a new landmass, destroyed many houses and left thousands homeless.

8 Autonomy

In 1976 the Azores became an autonomous region of Portugal, with its own government. However, Lisbon still controls education, health, and the army, police and judiciary. The Azores' president resides in Ponta Delgada.

9 Whaling Ban

Portugal's ratification of the Berne Convention on the Conservation of European Wildlife and Natural Habitats in 1982 banned whale hunting in the Azores. Today, it is among the world's best whale-watching destinations (see pp16–17).

10 Recognized by UNESCO

In 2004, Pico's famous vineyards (see pp32–3) were declared a UNESCO World Heritage Site, thanks to the island's unique wine-making traditions. It joined Angra do Heroísmo (see pp20–21), which was added to UNESCO's list in 1983.

TOP 10 HISTORIC FIGURES

Manuel de Arriaga

1 Thomas Hickling (1745–1834)
American merchant who built a summer residence in gardens that later became the Parque Terra Nostra (see p18).

2 John Bass Dabney (1766–1826)
Patriarch of the Dabney family (see p26) and first US consul to the Azores.

3 António José Severim de Noronha (1792–1860)
Count of Vila Flor, Noronha commanded the Liberal armies and secured victory against the Absolutists at Vila da Praia.

4 Carlos Machado (1828–1901)
An eminent naturalist, Machado created the Azorean Museum (see p41) in 1876, which was renamed in his honour.

5 Manuel de Arriaga (1840–1917)
The first elected President of the Republic of Portugal was born in Horta. A museum (see p26) celebrates his life.

6 Francisco de Lacerda (1869–1934)
Composer noted for his affinity for traditional Azorean music. A museum (see p92) houses personal artifacts.

7 Ernesto Canto da Maia (1890–1981)
Sculptor and vanguard of Portuguese Modernist art. His work is on display at the Museu Carlos Machado's (see p41) Núcleo de Santa Bárbara.

8 Natália Correia (1923–1993)
A poet and social activist, Correia wrote the lyrics of the Hino dos Açores (Hymn of the Azores), the regional anthem.

9 Berta Cabral (1952–present)
The first woman to lead a political party in the Azores; Cabral was elected head of the Social Democratic Party in 2008.

10 Ana Luis (1976–present)
Luis became the first female speaker of a regional assembly when she was elected President of the Assembly of the Azores in 2012.

TOP 10 Churches and Chapels

Altarpiece of Igreja do Colégio

17th century, the church is a picture of sculptured harmony and its façade brims with twirling flourishes of lava stone embellished with floral motifs.

3 Igreja de Santa Bárbara

Nestled amid verdant gardens overlooking the sea, the idyllic location is reason enough to visit this beautiful church (see p89). But the real eye-opener is its gilded Baroque interior. The focus is a richly carved retable and the polished panels of *azulejos* (tiles) illustrating the story of Santa Bárbara.

1 Igreja do Colégio

An exuberant façade hints at the rich interior of this early-17th-century church (see p13). A carved altarpiece of majestic proportions, dazzling in its Baroque ornamentation, remains partially gilded after the Jesuits were expelled in 1760. Colourful tiled panels under an arch depict Eucharistic allegories.

4 Igreja da Misericórdia

MAP V4 ▪ Pátio da Alfândega, Angra do Heroísmo, Terceira ▪ Open 10am–1pm & 2–5pm Mon–Fri, 1–5pm Sat, 4–6pm Sun

One of the Azores' most recognized religious buildings, this 18th-century church (see p20) stands on the site of a hospital, built in 1492 and the first in the Azores. A guided tour highlights the church's rich patrimony, brilliant acoustics and the damage caused by the 1980 earthquake (see p79).

2 Igreja de Nossa Senhora da Purificação

MAP F2 ▪ Santo Espírito, Santa Maria

According to local legend, this 16th-century church is linked to the first Holy Spirit festivals (see p62) in the Azores. Enlarged in the

Igreja de Nossa Senhora da Purificação

5 Igreja de São Boaventura

MAP R5 ▪ Rua do Hospital, Santa Cruz das Flores, Flores

The mustard-coloured façade is a landmark, and it is worth exploring the interior of this 17th-century

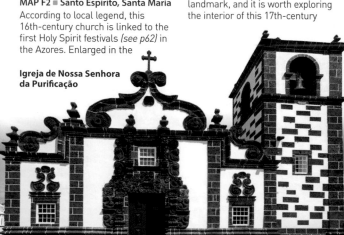

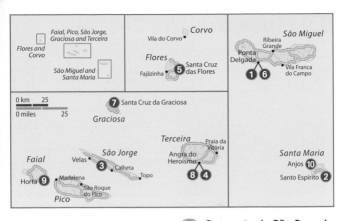

building. An extension of the Baroque Convento de São Boaventura, now a museum (see p40), the church's highlight is the vaulted cedarwood ceiling festooned with botanical motifs and allegorical figures.

6 Convento e Santuário de Nossa Senhora da Esperança

The *santuário* (sanctuary) of the Convent of Our Lady of Hope (see p13) displays the Ecce Homo figure, adorned with a quintet of sacred art representing *Glory*, *Crown*, *Sceptre*, *Cords* and *Reliquary*. The standout piece is *Glory*, crafted from gold-plated platinum and encrusted

Wooden figurine of Ecce Homo

with 6,842 precious stones. The ritual of Senhor Santo Cristo dos Milagres (see p62) has close associations with this 16th-century statue.

7 Ermida da Nossa Senhora da Ajuda

MAP K5 ■ Santa Cruz da Graciosa, Graciosa ■ Closed to the public

Crowning the Monte da Ajuda (see p81) summit, this 16th-century fortress-style building has a façade of plastered masonry, chunky buttresses, cornices, frames and decorative elements in exposed basalt. A finger-like belfry gives it a lopsided perspective.

8 Convento de São Gonçalo

MAP U4 ■ Rua Gonçalo V. Cabral, Angra do Heroísmo, Terceira ■ Open 9:30–11:30am & 2–4:30pm Mon–Fri, 9am–noon Sat

Founded in 1545, the convent (see p20) is the oldest in Angra do Heroísmo and the largest in the Azores. The church is noted for its outstanding figured choir decorated in gilded wood. The filigree crucifix in the chancel is a splendid example of 17th-century silverwork.

9 Igreja de São Salvador

The late-17th-century São Salvador church (see p27) was originally part of a Jesuit college, which functioned until the Jesuits were expelled from Portugal in 1759. Gilded chapels and tiled panels embellish the interior.

10 Capela de Nossa Senhora dos Anjos

Anjos was Christopher Columbus' first landfall on his return from the Americas in 1493. Some of his crew are said to have offered prayers here (see p72). The chapel's triptych is believed to have originated from the caravel of Portuguese explorer Gonçalo Velho Cabral (see p69).

🔟 Museums

Viewing pavilion at the Museu do Vinho set over Pico's iconic vineyards

1 Museu do Vinho

Pico's wine and vineyard culture is explained at this engaging museum (see p32). Set within an old Carmelite convent, the main building overlooks a UNESCO-protected landscape of vines. An annexe houses a vintage winepress. Visitors can taste and buy Pico wines here.

2 Museu de Angra do Heroísmo

Curated with considerable flair and imagination, the collections of ethnography, armoury, painting, sculpture, transport and decorative art trace Terceira's evolution from the 15th to the 19th century. The museum (see p20) is housed in the old Convento de São Francisco, and the convent's splendid church interior is a rewarding detour.

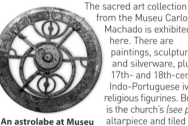

An astrolabe at Museu de Angra do Heroísmo

3 Museu da Horta

A former Jesuit college is home (see p26) to an exhibition that illustrates the island's history. Highlights include a section dedicated to Horta's 19th-century cable-telegraph stations and vintage bronze diving helmets. Do not miss the collection of fig tree pith sculptures (see p61), the largest of its kind in the world.

4 Casa dos Dabney

Three generations of Dabneys, a family from Boston, are chronicled at this museum-house. Influential in Horta business and social circles, the Dabneys established shipping and whaling enterprises, and also served as US consuls. The complex includes the Aquário de Porto Pim (see p27).

5 Núcleo de Arte Sacra – Igreja do Colégio

The sacred art collection from the Museu Carlos Machado is exhibited here. There are paintings, sculpture and silverware, plus 17th- and 18th-century Indo-Portuguese ivory religious figurines. But it is the church's (see p13) altarpiece and tiled panels that astound.

6 Museu das Flores

This ethnographic museum (see p100) explores the heritage of the island and its inhabitants' relationship with the land and the sea. The collection is displayed around an internal cloister of the enchanting Baroque Convento de São Boaventura.

7 Museu de Scrimshaw

The world's largest private collection of scrimshaw is on view in a room (see p26) above the well-known Peter Café Sport (see p96). Besides the remarkable engravings on whales' teeth, there are canes, cutlery, picture frames, needle boxes and other items shaped from whalebone.

8 Museu Carlos Machado

MAP V1 ▪ Rua Dr Carlos Machado, Ponta Delgada, São Miguel ▪ (296) 202 930 ▪ Open Apr–Sep: 10am–5:30pm Tue–Sun; Oct–Mar: 9:30am–5pm Tue–Sun ▪ Adm (under 15s free) ▪ www.museucarlosmach ado.azores.gov.pt

Centred around three permanent exhibitions, this outstanding museum (see p13) is housed in the 16th-century Convento de Santo André. The bird hall contains fine examples of the taxidermist's art and species include the now-extinct Carolina parakeet.

Sta Teresinha, Museu dos Baleeiros

9 Museu dos Baleeiros

The Whalers' Museum (see p91) provides an insight into whaling in the Azores until 1987. The exhibitions are set within three original 19th-century boathouses and displayed around the *Sta. Teresinha*, a restored traditional whaling boat. Exhibits include tools, handcrafted harpoons and fine examples of scrimshaw.

10 Museu da Graciosa

A contemporary wing provides a dramatic contrast against the original museum (see p81), housed in a late 19th-century building. Traditional farming tools, costumes, earthenware, an old winepress and period furniture form the exhibition. Look out for the annexed Barracão dos Botes Baleeiros, an old whaler's boathouse.

TOP 10 RARE OR UNUSUAL EXHIBITS IN AZOREAN MUSEUMS

1 Núcleo de Arte Sacra – Igreja do Colégio
The two paintings of the *Coroação da Virgem* (Coronation of the Virgin) by Vasco Pereira Lusitano (1535–1609).

2 Museu Carlos Machado
The Cedro do Mato, a 4,000-year-old cedar wood branch found on a mountain during construction of the Sete Cidades tunnel in the 1930s.

3 Museu de Angra do Heroísmo
The 1893-built "Paper Boat", a wooden-ribbed vessel, lined with layers of glued newspaper and coated with canvas.

4 Museu das Flores
An early 20th-century folding marine chair created entirely out of the jawbone of a sperm whale.

5 Museu dos Baleeiros
Beautifully carved and engraved nautilus conch shell, illustrated with pastoral scenes.

6 Museu do Vinho
The "Aroma" game. Activate an aroma from a cylinder and match it to various fruits, vegetables and condiments.

7 Museu da Horta
The headstone from the grave of the first settler and captain-major of Faial, Josse van Huerter (1430–95).

8 Museu de Scrimshaw
A solid lump of ambergris, produced in the digestive system of sperm whales. It is used widely in making perfumes.

9 Casa dos Dabney
The diary of Rose Dabney Forbes (1864–1947), an illuminated manuscript and a calligraphic triumph. Only 15 copies of it were printed.

10 Museu da Graciosa
Figurehead, probably representing Venus, carved from a single block of pine wood (c.1850–1900), salvaged from the schooner *Julia*.

Figurehead, Museu da Graciosa

🔟 Natural Wonders

1 Montanha do Pico
At 2,351 m (7,713 ft) Pico is the highest mountain (see pp88–9) in Portugal. The majestic sweep of this dormant stratovolcano's conical out-line is one of the archipelago's most iconic symbols. Capping the pit crater at the top is a volcanic cone, which forms the mountain's summit.

The rugged landscape of Capelinhos

2 Capelinhos
Bleak and austere, Capelinhos (see pp28–9) on Faial still bears the scars from a series of powerful earthquakes and volcanic eruptions that took place in 1957–8. The well-documented calamity reshaped the island and is regarded as a seminal volcanic event. Today the lunar-style landscape, replete with a lighthouse and a superb interpretative centre, is an evocative landmark.

3 Algar do Carvão
The largest concentration of amorphous silica stalactites in the world can be found deep within this volcanic cave system (see pp30–31) in Terceira. The mesmerizing interior is reached by descending a near-vertical 45-m (147-ft) vent. At the bottom of the 80-m (262-ft) lava tube is a lake fed by rainwater.

4 Lagoa das Furnas
Set in the Vale das Furnas, São Miguel's second-largest crater lake (see p19) is surrounded by forest-covered slopes. On the northern shore are hot water springs or fumaroles, known locally as caldeiras. The traditional cozido das Furnas (see p55) is cooked by locals in the hot earth here.

5 Furna do Enxofre
Graciosa's impressive caldera includes the Furna do Enxofre cave (see p78). The cavern features a huge domed ceiling – a rare volcanic phe-nomenon. The floor is reached by descending a concrete spiral staircase. A wide lake occupies the deepest recesses of the cave. Graciosa itself is a UNESCO Biosphere Reserve.

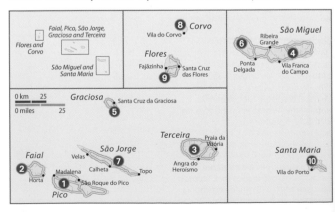

The picturesque Lagoa das Sete Cidades surrounded by lush greenery

6 Lagoa das Sete Cidades

Sunk within the verdant perimeter of an ancient caldera, the twin lakes *(see pp14–15)* – Lagoa Verde and Lagoa Azul (the Green Lake and the Blue Lake) – have a compelling charm. The Vista do Rei viewpoint overlooks the São Miguel landscape.

7 Fajã dos Cubres

Recognized by UNESCO as biosphere reserves, São Jorge's *fajãs* (coastal plains created from lava flows or collapsing cliffs) are areas of outstanding natural beauty. One of the most celebrated is Fajã dos Cubres *(see p89)* on the northern coast. A lagoon serves as a rich wetland habitat for a fascinating and diverse range of flora and fauna.

8 Caldeirão

Twin lakes dotted with tiny islets enhance the romantic character of this crater *(see p100)*, a 300-m (984-ft) deep caldera with a 2-km (1-mile) diameter. Singular in its appeal, the remoteness of Corvo – a UNESCO Biosphere Reserve – only adds to the crater's mystique.

9 Rocha dos Bordões

Rising from a weathered escarpment, this unique rock formation *(see p101)* with huge vertical basalt columns resembles a prehistoric pipe organ. It is a standout geological feature of Flores, which is a UNESCO Biopshere Reserve. The solidified folds appear to change colour with the sun's trajectory.

10 Deserto Vermelho dos Açores

An amazing anomaly known locally as Barreiro da Faneca, the "Red Desert of the Azores" *(see p69)* is an undulating arid landscape of rust-coloured clayish soil that blankets an age-old basaltic lava flow. The oxidized terrain is unlike any other found in the archipelago and is a protected Santa Maria geosite.

Deserto Vermelho dos Açores

🔟 Natural Swimming Pools and Thermal Springs

Caldeira Velha's mineral-rich waterfall

1 Caldeira Velha
MAP D5 ▪ Nr Ribeira Grande, São Miguel

Tucked away on the northern slopes of Lagoa do Fogo (see p68) is this idyllic bathing spot. A warm-water waterfall, rich in minerals, runs between lichen- and moss-coated boulders into a pond under a canopy of royal fern. There are changing rooms and picnic tables on site.

2 Biscoitos
Carved out of jagged, age-old basalt, the shallow pools at Biscoitos (see p78) are among the most beautiful on Terceira. Float in calm, crystalline waters and revel in the spray as a wayward Atlantic roller thunders into the rocks creating an instant salt-laced shower.

Natural pool at Biscoitos

3 Ponta da Ferraria
MAP A5 ▪ São Miguel ▪ Spa: adm ▪ www.termasferraria.com

A natural swimming pool formed of solidified lava, the salt water is heated by a bubbling spring. Crashing waves cool it enough for a relaxing dip. The neighbouring spa offers a more sophisticated wellbeing experience.

4 Poça da Dona Beija
This thermal spring complex (see p19) has five Jacuzzi-like bathing areas, each one fed by the warm waters Furnas is famous for. Changing rooms, hot and cold showers, and lockers are among the amenities. Arrive after dark and the whole place is fantastically illuminated.

5 Santa Cruz das Flores
MAP R5 ▪ Flores

Knee-deep in places when the tide is out, the water here is comfortably warm in summer. A basalt ridge tames the surf so it pours gently into the pools. A short stroll from Santa Cruz town centre, this is a prime sunbathing spot for locals.

6 Criação Velha
MAP L2 ▪ Nr Madalena, Pico

When swimming here on a sunny morning, Faial, across the channel, looks close enough to touch. This collection of green pools is protected from the restless sway of the Atlantic waves by craggy black lava clusters.

7 Calheta

Kids will enjoy the water slide built over the edge of this attractive natural pool at Calheta (see p92). On cloudless days the dramatic cone of Montanha do Pico (see p42) is clearly visible.

The muddy waters of Piscina de Água

8 Piscina de Água – Parque Terra Nostra

The muddy water should not deter visitors: the thermal spring supplying the pool contains essential minerals, flowing in at 35–40° C (95–104° F) temperature. Surrounded by botanical gardens (see p18), this iron-rich oasis works wonders on tired muscles.

9 Varadouro

MAP H2 ▪ Nr Ribeira do Cabo, Faial

This wide, irregular-shaped pool is enclosed but for a half-submerged tunnel bored into the wall, designed to channel the ocean's swell. An adjacent toddlers' pool makes Varadouro ideal for families.

10 Carapacho

Ideal for snorkelling, the natural rock pools here (see p79) are partly enclosed by a concrete breakwater. A bonus is the annexed swimming pool heated by the therapeutic waters from the nearby Carapacho Spa, renowned for its treatments for skin disorders and rheumatism.

TOP 10 BEACHES

1 Praia de Água d'Alto
MAP D6 ▪ Nr Vila Franca do Campo, São Miguel
A wide swathe of sand overlooked by hotel Pestana Bahia Praia (see p113).

2 Praia de Santa Bárbara
MAP C5 ▪ Ribeira Grande, São Miguel
A long boardwalk serves this sizeable beach preferred by surfers. Amenities include a pool complex and a restaurant.

3 Praia do Pópulo
MAP C6 ▪ Nr Lagoa, São Miguel
East of Ponta Delgada (see pp12–13), this "popular" beach lives up to its name.

4 Praia da Formosa
MAP E2 ▪ Santa Maria
Formosa is endowed with a band of soft white sand, rare in the Azores.

5 Praia de Angra do Heroísmo
MAP U4 ▪ Terceira
A city beach upgraded and expanded, this slither of sand is a family favourite.

6 Praia da Vitória
MAP P5 ▪ Terceira
The marina and sweeping promenade lend this place a resort-like ambience.

7 Praia
MAP K5 ▪ Graciosa
Praia's light sandy beach is wrapped around a sheltered bay.

8 Praia do Almoxarife
MAP K3 ▪ Nr Facho, Faial
This picturesque black-sand half-moon beach is a high-season hit.

9 Praia Fajã Grande
MAP Q6 ▪ Flores
Secluded beach set against a splendid backdrop of cascading waterfalls.

10 Praia do Porto Pim
MAP T4 ▪ Faial
Close to Horta's town centre, the beach lies under Monte da Guia (see p27).

The sweep of Praia do Porto Pim

TOP 10 Walks and Hikes

The Boca do Inferno viewpoint from where Sete Cidades can be seen

1 Lagoa do Canário–Sete Cidades–Mosteiros

MAP B5–A4 ■ São Miguel

The 14-km (9-mile) walk begins at Lagoa do Canário in Carvão. Marvel at the panorama from Miradouro da Boca do Inferno and then stroll along the northeastern rim of Caldeira das Sete Cidades *(see pp14–15)*. The route descends into Mosteiros on the coast.

2 Serra Branca–Praia

MAP J6–K5 ■ Graciosa

A picturesque amble, the trail begins in Serra Branca, crossing the island from west to east. Gentle on the legs, the 7-km (4-mile) trek will take around 2 hours, more if walkers go around the rim of the *caldeira*.

3 Montanha do Pico

The ascent of Pico *(see pp88–9)* is an ambition of many hikers visiting the Azores. Reaching the summit of Portugal's highest mountain is

The summit of Montanha do Pico

rewarded with stunning views of the surrounding islands. The trail begins at Cabeço das Cabras reception centre 1,200 m (4,000 ft) up the mountain.

4 Vila do Porto–Baía da Praia

MAP E2 ■ Santa Maria

The 16th-century Forte de Sao Brás *(see p72)* marks the starting point of a moderate 3-hour, 11-km (7-mile) walk that skirts the coast towards Praia da Formosa. Landmarks include the volcanic hillock of Facho de Vila and Fonte do Mourato village.

5 Serreta–Ponta do Raminho

MAP L5–4 ■ Terceira

From Serreta village *(see p80)* and following a well-trodden path through a bucolic landscape, this 10-km (6-mile) circuit takes around 4 hours to complete. Explore Reserva Florestal de Recreio da Mata da Serreta en route.

6 Caldeirinhas–Norte Grande

MAP N1–P1 ■ São Jorge

This route commences 700 m (2,300 ft) above sea level, so check the weather forecast beforehand. The 15-km (9-mile) trail along the spine of the island follows the central ridge to Pico da Esperança, the highest summit on São Jorge, before making a descent towards the coast. Admire breathtaking views along the way.

⑦ Caldeira–Capelinhos
MAP G2–H2 ▪ Faial

Known as the *Trilho dos Dez Vulcões*
(Ten Volcanoes Trail), this *(see p29)*
is an exhilarating 8-hour, 20-km
(12-mile) hike. Occasionally difficult,
the route snakes up from the Centro
de Interpretação do Vulcão dos
Capelinhos through impressive
scenery towards the *caldeira*.

⑧ Lajedo–Fajã Grande–Ponta Delgada

Europe's westernmost hiking trail,
the scenic 22-km (14-mile) course
(see p99) offers a stark contrast
between coast and countryside. It
passes geological wonders such as
Rocha dos Bordões *(see p43)*. The
distance can be covered in a day,
but many choose to undertake the
journey in two stages, or prefer to
start their walk from Ponta Delgada.

Walking track between fields on Pico

⑨ São Roque do Pico–Ladeira dos Moinhos
MAP N2 ▪ Pico

A circular route of a little over 3 km
(2 miles) beginning and ending in São
Roque do Pico, this walk takes in a
cobbled footpath and six watermills.
The gentle incline reveals pleasant
views of the town and the coast.

⑩ Vila do Corvo–Caldeirão
MAP R4 ▪ Corvo

The smallest and most remote
island of the archipelago is best
explored on foot. This moderate
4-km (2-mile) jaunt takes hikers
from the harbour at Vila do Corvo
to the edge of the Caldeirão, which
features two beautiful lakes.

TOP 10 IMPRESSIVE VIEWPOINTS

Miradouro Caldeira do Faial

1 Miradouro Caldeira do Faial
MAP H2 ▪ Faial
Marvel at breathtaking views of a
400-m (1,300-ft) deep and 1,500-m
(5,000-ft) wide crater from here.

2 Miradouro de Santa Iría
MAP D5 ▪ São Miguel
Scenic clifftop views are accompanied
by calls of Cory's shearwaters *(see p53)*.

3 Miradouro da Macela
MAP E2 ▪ Santa Maria
The outlook embraces Praia village, its
white-sand beach and the bay beyond.

4 Miradouro do Raminho
MAP L4 ▪ Terceira
Steep cliffs, headlands created from
lava flows and the Farol da Serreta lighthouse are included in the panorama.

5 Miradouro do Pico Timão
MAP J5 ▪ Graciosa
Admire the Serra Branca pastures from
the island's second-highest point.

6 Miradouro da Fajã do Ouvidor
MAP P1 ▪ São Jorge
On clear days inspiring sea views are
enhanced by a glimpse of Graciosa.

7 Miradouro de São Miguel Arcanjo
MAP N3 ▪ Pico
The quaint village of Prainha sits
against a wild seascape.

8 Miradouro da Vista do Rei
MAP A5 ▪ São Miguel
The main viewpoint of the island
overlooks both lakes of Sete Cidades.

9 Miradouro da Fajãzinha
MAP Q6 ▪ Flores
This lookout offers a spectacular vista
of the scenic Ribeira Grande valley.

10 Miradouro Caldeirão
MAP R4 ▪ Corvo
You're likely to have this superb
crater-lakes view all to yourself.

Following pages A slipper lobster spotted in waters off the Santa Maria coast

🔟 Outdoor Activities

A bottlenose dolphin off Faial

1 Diving and Snorkelling
Espírito Azul: www.espirito
azul.com

Crystalline waters, a rich marine eco-system and a seabed of volcanic caves and tunnels make the Azores one of Europe's most fascinating diving destinations (see pp24–5). Around 28 species of cetaceans, five types of sea turtles and over 600 fish species can be spotted in waters off the islands.

2 Canoeing and Kayaking
Azores For All: www.azores
forall.com

Exploring the islands' crater lakes (see pp14–15) by canoe is a beguiling experience. Paddling under the rim of a volcano is an awe-inspiring activity. Sea kayaking offers access to hidden grottoes, islets and stacks.

3 Whale Watching
Espaço Talassa: www.espaco
talassa.com

Over a third of the world's 80 or so cetacean species have been sighted in the Azores, a global hot spot for whale and dolphin watching

Whale watching off Pico

(see pp16–17). From early April to late June daily sightings of these majestic mammals are almost guaranteed. The sperm whale is present all year.

4 Surfing
Azores Surf Center: www.
azoressurfcenter.com

This is an activity that can be enjoyed throughout the year, although surfing conditions in winter are influenced by swells from the north, persistent depressions and cold fronts. Summer is dominated by waves from the south whipped up by tropical storms. The surf schools on São Miguel are professionally run and highly regarded.

5 Walking and Hiking
Aventour – Azores Adventures:
www.aventour.pt

Following the trails (see pp46–7) that crisscross the nine islands is one of the most rewarding ways to get to know the Azores. Amble inland for magnificent cloud-scudded peaks, verdant valleys and ancient craters that cup tranquil lakes. Lining the coast are steep sea cliffs, shallow lagoons and mysterious lava plains.

6 Bird Watching
Gerby Birding: www.gerby
birding.com

The Azores are globally recognized as a prime bird-watching destination for several species (see pp52–3). Ornithologists and "twitchers" flock to the islands to spot scarce residents such as the Azores bullfinch and Monteiro's storm petrel. The autumn migration is a particularly rewarding period, especially on Flores and Corvo.

7 Cycling and Mountain Biking

Azores MTB: www.azoresmtb.com

Riding around the Azores takes visitors through quiet country lanes and rolling pastures. Freewheel the coast and discover natural rock pools and beaches (see pp44–5).

8 Canyoning

WestCanyon: www.west canyon.pt

Wading through streams and abseiling down waterfalls and canyons appeals to many outdoor adventurers. São Miguel, São Jorge and especially remote Flores are preferred locations for this activity.

Canyoning down a steep cliff

9 Horse Riding

Quinta da Terça: www.quinta daterca.com

Saddle up and tour the islands on horseback (see p82). Trotting down trails along the coast or through laurel forests is amazing. Many hotels combine a stay with equestrian activities.

10 Sailing

Pure Sail Azores: www.pure sailazores.com

Navigating the archipelago by yacht is exhilarating, almost akin to following in the footsteps of earlier Portuguese explorers (see p36). First-rate marina infrastructure plus numerous sheltered bays and inlets provide safe havens along the way.

TOP 10 SPECIAL INTEREST ACTIVITIES

Batalha golf course, São Miguel

1 Golfing
www.azoresgolfislands.com
There's a choice of three courses: Batalha and Furnas on São Miguel, and Terceira.

2 Climbing and Rappelling
www.bootla.pt
Climb and descend geological wonders under expert supervision.

3 Hot Air Ballooning
www.exploreterceira.com
Float over breathtaking volcanic scenery in perfect weather conditions.

4 Paragliding
www.asassaomiguel.com
An annual paragliding festival is held in August at Sete Cidades (see pp14–15).

5 Geotourism
www.naturfactor.com
Go underground with speleologists for tours of Pico's caves and grottoes.

6 Big Game Fishing
www.sportfishingazores.com
The fishing season runs from July to mid-October. Fish quotas are regulated.

7 Coasteering
www.azoreanactiveblueberry.com
Explore the water's edge by scrambling over, climbing up or swimming along a rocky, sometimes cut-off coastline.

8 Health and Wellbeing
Termas do Carapacho: (295) 714 212
Soak in mineral-rich waters to ease rheumatism and skin disorders.

9 Stand-up Paddleboarding (SUP)
www.garoupa.pt
SUP on the crater lakes or the sea and discover picturesque coves and grottoes.

10 Jet Skiing
www.ontravelazores.com
The aquatic "motorbike" provides an adrenaline rush for watersports enthusiasts with a need for speed.

⏫ Birdlife

A flock of roseate terns catching fish from the ocean off Graciosa

1 Azores Bullfinch

Distinguished by its black cap, face, wings and tail, this diminutive bird, known locally as *priolo*, is the most threatened and second-rarest passerine in Europe. It is endemic to the Azores but confined solely to São Miguel, specifically between Serra da Tronqueira *(see p70)* and Vale das Furnas in the eastern region.

2 Monteiro's Storm Petrel

This is the smallest seabird found in the archipelago. Identified by its broad wings, square tail and prominent diagonal wing bar, the species breeds only on two islets off Graciosa: Ilhéu de Baixo and Ilhéu da Praia *(see p83)*, considered the largest colony of these birds in the world with approximately 100 pairs.

3 Azores Grey Wagtail

These lively and inquisitive birds, known for habitually flicking their tails in a characteristic bobbing motion, thrive across all habitats here – they have even been spotted near the summit of Pico. The male of this endemic subspecies can be identified by its black throat; the female's is white.

Azores grey wagtail

4 Roseate Tern

A sleek, handsome seabird with long tail-streamers, this is a summer migrant and is seen throughout the Azores from April to July, when it breeds. Nesting is most abundant on Santa Maria, Graciosa and Flores *(see p99)*, particularly on islets such as Ilhéu de Maria Vaz.

5 Atlantic Canary

Vivid yellow-green plumage with chestnut-brown streaks identifies this small passerine, one of the most colourful in the Azores. Known also as the island canary or wild canary, it is common on all the islands.

6 Common Buzzard

A subspecies endemic to the Azores, this is the archipelago's only resident bird of prey. Smaller than its mainland counterpart, it can be seen in coastal areas and mountainous regions, except the Western Group of islands. Early settlers mistook this bird for a goshawk, which is *açor* in Portuguese, or in plural *açores*. Hence came the collective name for the nine islands *(see p36)*.

7 Azores Quail

Patience and luck are required to spot this shy ground-nesting game bird, which breeds in meadows and fields. The tiny Azores quail is a resident bird native to the archipelago and is commonly sighted on Terceira (see p82). It is often heard rather than seen, the distinctive quick-fire "wet-my-lips" call emanating from tall grass or cereal fields.

8 Goldcrest

Out of the three endemic subspecies in the Azores it is the Santa Maria goldcrest (see p73) that has captured ornithologists' imagination. The smallest bird in Europe, the goldcrest is restless and hyperactive. The orange crown of the male and the lemon-yellow crest of the female provide bright contrast against the olive-green tones of their upperparts.

9 Cory's Shearwater

One of the strangest sounds likely to be heard during summer nights in the Azores is the constricted, gurgling call of the Cory's shearwater. The birds are seen between March and mid-November, and their raucous cackling marks the breeding season, when they nest in colonies on sea cliffs and rocky outcrops.

A Cory's shearwater taking flight

10 Atlantic Yellow-Legged Gull

The interisland ferries offer excellent vantage points from which to admire this heavy-set seabird, which has a loud nasal "laugh". Found in abundance on the archipelago, this bird can be easily spotted on landfills and pastureland. Bright yellow legs differentiate it from similar species such as lesser black-backed and herring gulls. Nesting season lasts from mid-March to early May.

TOP 10 ENDEMIC FLOWERING PLANTS

Azorean Bellflower

1 Azorean Bellflower (Azorina vidalii)
Rare coastal perennial found across the archipelago except Graciosa and Faial. Flowers May–October.

2 Azorean Holly (Ilex perado azorica)
Subspecies found on all islands except Graciosa. Dispersed in the laurel forest, normally above 500 m (1,600 ft).

3 Azorean Blueberry (Vaccinium cylindraceum)
Deciduous shrub with narrow leaves and red flowers. Found on all islands.

4 Azorean Laurustinus (Viburnum treleasei)
Diminutive evergreen shrub noted for its pinkish-white corolla. Blossoms in spring everywhere, except on Graciosa.

5 Azorean Heather (Erica azorica)
Embellished with flowers of green petals and shades of purple. Common on coastal cliffs up to 1,500 m (5,000 ft).

6 Azorean Ivy (Hedera azorica)
Evergreen climbing plant found in dense bush. Flowers are in small umbels.

7 Azorean Dwarf Mistletoe (Arceuthobium azoricum)
Found only on Graciosa, Pico, Faial and Terceira. Characterized by yellow-green stems and paired conical leaves.

8 Azorean Cherry (Prunus azorica)
Rare subspecies with scented flowers that look striking. Found on all islands, except Santa Maria, Graciosa, Flores and Corvo.

9 Oleaceae (Picconia azorica)
Evergreen shrub distinguished by a white corolla and ink-blue oval berries. Does not thrive on Graciosa.

10 Hochstetter's Butterfly Orchid (Platanthera micrantha)
Rare plant with pale yellow-green flowers found on all islands, except Graciosa. Seen mostly above 200 m (656 ft).

TOP 10 Traditional Azorean Cuisine

Flavourful *caldeirada de peixe*

1 Caldeirada de Peixe

The Azores are highly regarded for the variety of fish, and this stew can be made using a range of local species including grouper, bream and red snapper, as well as prawns and shellfish. Potato, onion, garlic, tomato, white wine and seasoning are also added.

2 Sopa do Espírito Santo

Soup of the Holy Spirit is prepared during the annual Festas do Espírito Santo celebrations (see p62). It is a delicious and hearty broth made using vegetables and meats, seasoned with mint, bay leaves and garlic. Thick slices of buttered cornbread soak up the flavours. Recipes differ from island to island, but the result is always ladled out from a huge tureen.

3 Pudim de Chá Verde dos Açores

Given that the Azores have the only tea estates in Europe, this chilled dessert is unique. It is made with green tea leaves harvested at Gorreana (see p68), and the recipe retains all the nutrients and anti-oxidants, despite the milk and sugar.

4 Sopa de Funcho

Simple and healthy, fennel soup is a flavoursome starter to many an Azorean meal. The whole plant is used, cut to bite-size pieces. Onion, potato, tomato and carrot lend weight. Some cooks add *feijão vermelho* (red beans) to thicken the texture.

5 Pudim de Queijo da Ilha

Soft, smooth and creamy, this heavenly pudding, or flan, is prepared using cheese from São Jorge, along with eggs, natural yogurt and a deliciously nutty caramel sauce. It is an ideal choice after a hearty dinner.

6 Alcatra

Emblematic of Terceira, this traditional pot roast is prepared using *alcatra* (rump) steak marinated in Vinho de Cheiro, a white wine from the Isabella grape. A key ingredient is smoked bacon. Seasoned with allspice and baked in a clay pot, this is one of the most aromatic Azorean dishes.

Alcatra in a clay pot

7 Lapas Grelhadas

Grilled *lapas* (limpets) are a traditional delicacy and can be enjoyed year-round. This dish is usually prepared as an appetizer, and baked with garlic and lemon juice. Another variation is *arroz de lapas* – risotto garnished with parsley. Santa Maria restaurants often serve *lapas de molho Afonso* – braised limpets in a spicy sauce.

***Lapas grelhadas*, made using limpets**

Locals preparing *cozido das Furnas*

8 Cozido das Furnas

Huge pots of *cozido* (stew) are lowered into the hot, volcanic ground next to the beautiful Lagoa das Furnas. After six hours of cooking in the earthy ovens, the pots – full of chicken, beef, pork, black pudding, kale, white cabbage, sweet potato, yam and carrot – are ceremoniously raised and sent to nearby restaurants, where the flavoursome assortment is served to diners *(see p19).*

9 Polvo Guisado

Octopus stewed with wine, onions and red-pepper paste, this is one of the archipelago's most representative culinary specialities. Each island has its own variation, with oven roast potatoes also finding room on the plate. Either way, it is a beautifully textured, rich and appetizing seafood dish.

10 Morcela com Ananás

An Azorean staple, the classic prepandial black pudding with pineapple is an inspired combination. The "pudding" is, in fact, grilled blood sausage. It can be sliced broadly and topped with the caramelized fruit, or offered cubed and skewered cocktail-style. Another variation is a flower presentation where a ring of pineapple, sculpted as petals, surrounds a circular slice of sausage.

TOP 10 WINES AND LIQUEURS

1 Arinto dos Açores by António Maçanita
António Maçanita, highly regarded for his mainland Alentejo wines, created this punchy Pico white *(see pp32–3).*

2 Cancela do Porco
Balanced acidity holds the flavours of this white, made from Verdelho grapes grown on Pico *(see pp32–3).*

3 Frei Gigante
Named after friar Pedro Gigante, this straw-coloured wine with a fruity flavour is a Pico island classic *(see pp32–3).*

4 Pedras Brancas
Several wines are available from this Graciosa estate, as well as *aguardente* (clear brandy or "fire water"), distilled in copper tanks *(see p81).*

5 Da Resistência Branca
Ripe and creamy with hints of honey and plum, this excellent white is pure Verdelho grape *(see p78).*

6 Chico Maria
Fortified sweet wine produced from Verdelho grapes. Available in dry, medium-dry and sweet styles *(see p77).*

7 Vinho Generoso
Individually numbered wine bottled in decorative stoneware fired and glazed by artist Renato Costa e Silva *(see p77).*

8 Aguardente Velhíssima Vínica Mulher de Capote
At a potent 40 per cent, this premier spirit is regarded as the best "fire water" in the Azores *(see p71).*

9 Maracuja Gourmet
Passion fruit liqueur noted for its pleasant aroma and intense flavour. A favourite island-wide tipple *(see p71).*

10 Queen of the Islands
A luxuriously smooth and creamy liqueur made with milk from the islands and flavoured with anisette *(see p71).*

A range of Azorean liqueurs

🔟 Restaurants

1 Ti Choa
This welcoming restaurant (see p85) serves generous portions of rich and delicious dishes, such as *molho de fígado* (marinated pork with liver). Try the tasting menu if you're having trouble choosing.

2 Rotas da Ilha Verde
The creative cuisine served at this restaurant (see p75) is fresh and totally vegetarian. Its inventive menu includes dishes such as the mouth-watering artichoke risotto and crispy green salad. Considered one of the best vegetarian options in the entire archipelago, this place features vintage furniture and offbeat decor.

3 Genuíno
Owner Genuíno Madruga, the acclaimed Portuguese yachtsman who has twice circumnavigated the globe solo, often regales diners with tales of his high sea exploits. The popular restaurant (see p97) displays the memorabilia collected during his voyages, and the menu has a suitably nautical flavour. Admire the lovely views of Porto Pim from here.

4 Anfiteatro
Contemporary cuisine is prepared with pizzazz at this waterfront venue (see p75). The seasonal menu honours traditional Azorean cuisine but draws on modern techniques and international flavours. The wine list offers some

A pork dish served at Anfiteatro

of the grandest labels in Portugal. Anfiteatro also hosts the prestigious "10 Fest" gourmet food festival.

5 Cais da Angra
The unbeatable location (see p85) overlooking the marina is accentuated by huge picture windows. Highly regarded for its cuts of tender meat, including a delicious porterhouse, and grilled Aberdeen Angus rib with burnt cream.

6 Pôr do Sol
Built from basalt stone, this evocative farmhouse restaurant (see p103) set in rolling pastureland is the epitome of rustic. Decorated with antique ceramics, iron pots and pans and the odd farming implement, this is the place to sample home-style cuisine – rich hearty food served up on glazed earthenware plates.

Charming, rustic exterior of Pôr do Sol

⑦ Ancoradouro

The "anchorage" is a seafood hot spot *(see p97)* offering fine dining in a boathouse-like setting. The menu lists a veritable ocean harvest, cuisine best sampled on the basalt terrace, which offers a panorama of Faial across the channel. Order the *espetada de peixe* (fish kebab) and muse over the arm-long wine list.

⑧ Fornos de Lava

The mouthwatering traditional Azorean fare served here *(see p97)* is the creation of the founder, a Galician chef. The menu features home-style meat and fish dishes, accompanied by fresh, organically grown vegetables. On clear days, the restaurant affords magnificent views of neighbouring Pico and Faial.

The colourful dining room at Alcides

⑨ Alcides

This noted family-run restaurant *(see p75)* has been dishing up *bife à Alcides* – prime steak garnished with red pepper and garlic – since it opened in 1955. Tables are set against scarlet walls under a vaulted lava-stone ceiling. A huge canvas by celebrated local artist Domingos Rebelo enriches the decor.

⑩ Fonte Cuisine

Part of Aldeia da Fonte *(see p113)*, this restaurant serves signature Azorean cuisine in tranquil surroundings *(see p97)*. The menu features well-crafted local dishes such as *lapas grelhadas (see p54)* and an excellent wine list.

TOP 10 CAFÉS AND BARS

Quirky wall decor at 3/4 Café

1 3/4 Café
This unpretentious, graffiti-walled café-bar *(see p74)* serves snacks by day before turning up the music at night.

2 Casa de Chá e Bar
Faial's very own Japanese teahouse *(see p96)* serves over 100 varieties of tea in a hidden back garden in Horta.

3 Sports One Café
MAP U2 ▪ Ponta Delgada, São Miguel ▪ (296) 308 500
Pool tables and TV screens furnish Hotel Talisman's *(see p116)* English-style pub.

4 Chaminé Club
MAP E2 ▪ São Pedro Vila do Porto, Santa Maria ▪ (917) 212 490
This fashionable nightclub and music bar starts warming up after midnight.

5 Birou Bar
The centrally located Birou Bar *(see p84)* is known for its origami ceiling decor.

6 Pub Bar Vila Sacramento
Hugely popular, this nightspot *(see p84)* is also known as the Good Music Club after its much-admired DJ sets.

7 The Gin Library
Stylish but cosy bar *(see p74)* serving a superlative collection of gins, including Baleia Gin, created by the owner.

8 Cella Bar
Set on the coast, the lovely Cella Bar *(see p97)* received an international design award for its stylish architecture.

9 Peter Café Sport
This place *(see p96)* is world famous for one drink: the coveted gin and tonic mixed with passion fruit juice.

10 Lucino's
Open all day for snacks and light meals, Lucino's *(see p103)* livens up after dark.

🔟 Places to Shop

1 Cooperativa de Artesanato de Santa Maria

MAP F2 ■ Santo Espírito, Santa Maria ■ (296) 884 888 ■ Closed Sat (from 2pm) & Sun

The artisans of this historic cooperative are renowned throughout the Azores for their weaving skills. On most days nimble-fingered women can be seen creating beautifully patterned bedspreads and blankets. Their hand-woven costumes embody the island's rural character.

Blue-and-white ceramic plate

2 Adega A Buraca

MAP M2 ■ Estrada Regional 35, Santo António, Pico ■ (292) 642 119

Wines, brandies and liqueurs from across the islands, plus jams, breads, cheeses and biscuits are available at this farmhouse delicatessen (see p93). Traditionally styled, the rustic ambiance is complemented by the private museum brimming with antique farming tools and vintage machine parts.

3 Parque Atlântico

There are over 80 stores and boutiques, a food court and a multiplex cinema in this impressive shopping mall (see p71). The "Atlantic" theme is appropriately conveyed in the shape of an original whaling boat in full sail displayed on the ground floor.

4 Cerâmica Vieira

The Azores' only manufacturer of glazed pottery, Cerâmica Vieira (see p71) has been family-owned since its foundation in 1862. Visitors can watch the potters at work before browsing the outstanding tiles and tableware, with many pieces decorated in the traditional blue-and-white brushstroke style known as Louça da Lagoa.

5 Maria da Assunção Nunes de Azevedo

MAP R6 ■ Estrada Regional, Fazenda das Lajes, Flores ■ (292) 593 256

A much-loved local resident, Maria makes bouquets and rosettes from the dyed pith of hydrangeas. She also uses fish scales to shape equally exquisite blooms (see p60). Passed down from generation to generation, this is a skill she readily demonstrates to passers-by, and the dainty miniatures are all for sale.

6 Bordado dos Açores

Needlework of the highest order is produced at this studio (see p82) run by João Filho and his daughters. Ornate baby bibs, bread cloths and bottle aprons, all hand embroidered using traditional techniques, are available to purchase.

7 Loja Peter Café Sport

A preppy-nautical theme runs through the collection of apparel, branded with the café's (see p96) distinctive logo. Clothing includes T-shirts, jumpers and

Whaling boat at Parque Atlântico

windcheaters. Also on sale are posters taken from the famous photograph of "Neptune" during a storm – a monster wave crashing over a headland, the profile of which resembles the god of the sea.

8 Louvre Michaelense

The sense of nostalgia at this quaint, wood-lined emporium (see p71) is tangible. Old-fashioned glass-fronted wall cabinets are filled with teas, spices, local ceramics and handmade hats and handbags. Displays of tempting cakes and pastries line the counter. Pause for coffee or a light meal before purchasing one of their quirky souvenirs.

Vintage decor at Louvre Michaelense

9 Uniqueijo

Visitors do not have to join a guided tour of this cheese factory (see p92) to buy rich, aromatic São Jorge cheese, but doing so makes it much more fun. There are plenty of varieties on offer: from those aged for several months to the mature two-year-old special, which can be identified by its black label.

10 Adega e Cooperativa Agrícola da Ilha Graciosa

Graciosa's wine and agricultural cooperative (see p81) produces the much admired Pedras Brancas range of wines, notably the white VQPRD. Another favourite tipple is Angelica, but for a real kick try the Vínica, their robust aguardente. The estate also cultivates garlic and melon. All produce can be sampled and bought at the farmhouse store.

TOP 10 PLACES TO BUY REGIONAL BREADS, CAKES AND SWEETS

Traditional *queijadas do Pico*

1 Pastelaria e Padaria Linu: Pico
Queijadas do Pico
A regional variation of sweet *queijadas*, with goat's cheese adding a sour edge.

2 Vila Franca do Campo: São Miguel
Queijadas da Vila Franca
Cakes that originated in the 17th century from a recipe handed down by nuns.

3 Cooperativa de Artesanato de Santa Maria: Santa Maria
Biscoitos de Orelha
Rounded textured biscuits resembling the shape of an ear (*orelha*).

4 O Forno: Terceira
Bolos Dona Amélia
Spicy cakes topped with icing sugar. Named after Portugal's last queen.

5 Casa Museu João Tomáz Bettencourt: Graciosa
Pasteis de Arroz
Cakes made from rice and egg white and flavoured with almond (*see p81*).

6 Quejadas da Graciosa: Graciosa
Queijadas da Graciosa
Star-shaped, traditional version of the Portuguese *queijadas* pastry (*see p83*).

7 Pasteleria Dôcilha: São Jorge
Espécies de São Jorge
Ribbed cookies baked with *espécies* (spices) such as cinnamon and anise.

8 Dulçores: São Jorge
Rosquilhas de Aguardente
Flower-shaped delicacies in which *aguardente* is added to eggs and flour.

9 Aromas & Sabores: Pico
Bolo Baleeiro
Pico's very own whaler's cake, crammed full of honey with cinnamon flavours.

10 Café Atlântida: São Miguel
Bolos Lêvedos
Sweet, flat soft rolls. The best are made in Furnas (*see pp18–19*).

🔟 Arts and Crafts

1 Fish Scales

A handicraft passed down through generations, the art of turning fish scales into decorative flower clusters requires a high degree of skill. The scales are first dyed and then shaped into delicate petals or leaves with scissors. At the Escola Regional de Artesanato on Pico (see p93) visitors can watch the entire process and admire the colourful, palm-sized bouquets on display.

Decorative flowers made of fish scales

2 Lapinhas

These unique miniature nativity scenes are set within domes or glass boxes. Created using small figures of painted pottery, fragments of rock, tiny sea shells and moss, flowers and plants, these beautiful and intricate cribs first appeared on the archipelago in the 17th century.

3 Weaving

Using wool, linen or cotton, traditional weaving – which is still done on antique hand-worked looms across the Azores – is represented by the wonderful blankets, handbags and quilts produced at the Cooperativa de Artesanato Nossa Senhora da

Hand-woven traditional handicraft

Encarnação (see p92). The cooperative's ponto alto-style (relief stitch) bedspreads have their origins in the 16th century.

4 Ceramics and Earthenware

Contributing significantly to the Azorean cultural identity, the most emblematic traditional pottery includes simple unglazed pieces such as the bilha (clay jug) and alguidar (bowl). Founded in 1862, Cerâmica Vieira (see p71) is the only manufacturer of ceramic pottery in the Azores. Clay is moulded on the potter's wheel and everything is hand-painted.

5 Violas

Two heart-shaped soundholes distinguish the viola da terra as a unique Azorean musical instrument. The 12-string handmade guitar has a separate fingerboard inlaid in the soundboard, with the bridge ending in bird-like figures. The regional guitars of São Mateus and Santa Cruz on Graciosa are especially decorative.

6 Scrimshaw

Dating from the 19th century and synonymous with Azorean whaling heritage, scrimshaw refers to scroll-work and carvings created by whalers using the bones and teeth of whales. Once widely practised, the tradition has almost disappeared with the diminishing supply of whale teeth. It is now illegal to take scrimshaw and whalebone products out of Portugal. The Museu de Scrimshaw (see p26) has a collection of rare engraved examples on display.

7 Basalt Jewellery

An example of modern Azorean handicraft, jewellery incorporating basalt rock works both as a fashion accessory and as a symbolic element, like a talisman. Formed from the rapid cooling of basaltic lava, the rock's characteristic sooty hue and pitted texture complements the polished surface of gold or silver (see p71).

8 Corn Husk Dolls

Early settlers used wheat straw, wood and other plant matter as raw material to create various decorative artifacts. These included *bonecas de folhelho* – dolls crafted from cornhusks. Still made today, the beautiful figurines are indicative of the islands' agricultural heritage.

Dolls made from cornhusks

9 Fig Tree Pith Carvings

Incredible dexterity and patience are required to produce fig pith art. Using the soft, fragile pith tissue from the wild fig tree, skilled practitioners produce anything from delicate floral compositions to miniature caravels in full sail. Carvings can be seen on display at the Museu da Horta (see p26).

10 Embroidery

The style of embroidery varies between islands. *Matiz* stitchwork from São Miguel dates back to the early 1930s and has lovely blue floral and campestral motifs. On Terceira, look for pieces created using the exquisite Richelieu stitch. Faial is known for unusual wheat straw embroidery on black tulle.

TOP 10 SOUVENIRS

1 Wooden Door Locks
Rosa Mariana Mendonça: Caminho da Horta Funda, Corvo
Traditional wooden door locks carved by artisan and shop owner Rosa's father, José Mendonça de Inês.

2 Tea
Plantações de Chá Gorreana: Gorreana, São Miguel
Varieties of black and green teas from the only tea plantation in Europe.

3 Regional Sweets
Cooperativa de Artesanato de Santa Maria: Santo Espírito, Santa Maria
Homemade *biscoitos de orelha* and other goodies from the archipelago.

4 Ceramics
Azulart de Aurélia Rocha: Angra do Heroísmo, Terceira
Glazed pottery, such as wall clocks and decorated tiles, made by local artists.

5 Lacework
Associação de Artesãos da Ilha Graciosa: Santa Cruz, Graciosa
Hats, scarves and cowls fashioned from crochet, and embroidered tablemats.

6 Cheeses
Uniqueijo: Beira, São Jorge
Choice Azores cheeses, including Queijo São Jorge, the connoisseur's favourite.

7 Wines
Adega A Buraca: Santo António, Pico
Verdelho Original, a zesty white from the UNESCO-protected Pico vineyards.

8 Wickerwork
Centro de Artesanato do Capelo: Capelo, Faial
Traditional products for sale, including handmade wicker baskets.

9 Flowers From Hydrangea Piths
Maria da Assunção Nunes de Azevedo: Lajes, Flores
Locally made replica flower bouquets.

10 Soft Toy Whales
Louvre Michaelense: Ponta Delgada, São Miguel
Hand-stitched, cute and cuddly cetaceans in varied patterned fabrics.

Soft toy whale

🔟 Traditional Festivals

1 Festas do Espírito Santo
All islands ■ Every Sun for seven weeks after Easter

The archipelago's most important festivals are associated with the Espírito Santo (Holy Spirit). A villager is crowned *imperador* (emperor) and presides over the colourful cere-monies. On the seventh Sunday, soup *(see p54)* and bread are distributed from an *império* (chapel).

2 Senhor Santo Cristo dos Milagres
MAP U2 ■ São Miguel ■ 5th Sun after Easter

Ponta Delgada's celebration honouring the Lord Holy Christ of Miracles is the largest religious festival in the Azores. It is centred on the 16th-century Convento de Nossa Senhora da Esperança *(see p39)*, and features a town procession where the revered figure of Senhor Santo Cristo dos Milagres is carried over streets paved with a fabulous floral tableaux.

3 Festas Sanjoaninas
MAP M6 ■ Terceira ■ Nearest Friday to 24 Jun

Mirroring the Portuguese mainland's Festas dos Santos Populares (Festivals of the Popular Saints) tradition, Terceira honours São João (St John) by hosting a huge costumed parade in Angra do Heroísmo *(see pp20–21)*. The dancing and singing draws on age-old customs and folklore.

4 Festa do Emigrante
MAP R6 ■ Lajes das Flores, Flores ■ 3rd weekend in Jul

While acknowledging the Holy Spirit with an allegorical procession, this festival is essentially a homecoming party for thousands of Azorean migrants who return to the islands for the summer break. Fringe events include literary talks, art exhibitions and sporting tournaments.

5 Festa da Senhora da Guia
MAP J3 ■ Horta, Faial ■ 1st Sun in Aug

A visual treat, the festival of Nossa Senhora da Guia (Protector of the Fishermen) gathers trawler crews from across the island to lead a procession from Porto Pim to the town centre. It marks the beginning of the Semana do Mar (Sea Week), essentially a yachting regatta, but festivities happen on land too.

6 Festival Ilha Branca
MAP J5 ■ Santa Cruz da Graciosa, Graciosa ■ 2nd week in Aug

As with many fêtes and galas in the Azores, the "White Island" festival merges the religious with the secular. Integrated into the parallel Holy Christ ceremonies, Graciosa lets its hair down with modern Portuguese music that attracts a predominantly young crowd.

Vibrant Festas Sanjoaninas parade

⑦ Festa da Nossa Senhora da Assunção

MAP E2 ▪ Santa Maria ▪ 15th Aug

Vila do Porto's *(see p68)* municipal gardens host this festival in which Santa Maria pays homage to its patron saint. Entertainment programmes are accompanied by religious ceremonies that take place in and around the Igreja de Nossa Senhora da Assunção.

⑧ Semana dos Baleeiros

MAP N3 ▪ Lajes do Pico, Pico ▪ Last week in Aug

The Week of the Whalers festival is linked to the worship of Nossa Senhora de Lourdes, the patron saint of whalers. This prestigious event features traditional *fado* music and modern guitar rock performances. However, it is the whaling boat regatta that captures the occasion's true spirit.

Whaling boat regatta, Pico

⑨ Romaria de Santo Cristo

MAP Q2 ▪ São Jorge ▪ 1st Sun in Sep

Romarias (religious pilgrimages) are an important tradition of the Catholic communities here. The Holy Christ procession in Fajã dos Vimes ends at the village's tiny chapel, Capela de São Sebastião, for a celebratory feast.

⑩ Festa da Senhora do Bom Caminho

MAP R4 ▪ Vila do Corvo, Corvo ▪ 2nd weekend in Sep

Announcing the arrival of autumn, this ceremony praises Our Lady of the Good Way, a reference to the figure of the Virgin, which is taken on a procession towards the caldera. Highlights include folk dancing, an open-air Mass and lots of food and wine.

TOP 10 SHOWS AND EVENTS

Red Bull cliff diving contest

1 Azores Trail Run
Faial ▪ May ▪ www.azorestrail run.com
Cross-country courses that include the 70-km (43-mile) Blue Island Challenge.

2 Red Bull Cliff Diving
São Miguel ▪ Early Jun ▪ www.redbullcliffdiving.com
High-octane extreme sports event.

3 10 Fest
São Miguel ▪ Mid-Jun ▪ www.taste. visit azores.com
Modern gourmet dishes prepared by ten chefs at Anfiteatro *(see p75)*.

4 Semana Cultural das Velas
São Jorge ▪ First week in Jul
Festival showcasing local writers, artists and musicians. It also hosts a yacht race.

5 Walk & Talk
São Miguel ▪ Mid-Jul ▪ www.walk talkazores.org
Cutting-edge urban art festival.

6 Santa Maria Blues
Santa Maria ▪ Mid-Jul ▪ www.santa mariablues.com
Highly regarded blues festival.

7 Taste in Adegas
Pico ▪ Mid-Jul
Wine tastings at *adegas* (wineries).

8 Grande Festival de Folclore da Relva – Mostra Folcrórica do Atlântico
São Miguel ▪ First week in Aug
One of the largest folklore festivals held in Relva every year.

9 Atlantis Cup
São Miguel, Santa Maria, Terceira, Faial ▪ First week in Aug
Prestigious sailing regatta that connects four islands in the Azores.

10 Angrajazz
Terceira ▪ Oct ▪ www.angrajazz.com
The archipelago's premier jazz festival.

Azores
Area by Area

The beautiful Lagoa do Fogo amid lush greenery, São Miguel

São Miguel and Santa
   Maria Islands   **66**

Terceira and Graciosa Islands   **76**

São Jorge, Pico and
   Faial Islands   **88**

Flores and Corvo Islands   **98**

▣ São Miguel and Santa Maria Islands

The largest and the most varied of the nine islands in the Azores, São Miguel offers an ideal introduction to this mid-Atlantic archipelago. Ponta Delgada, the island's principal town, is a cosmopolitan base for exploring the volcanic landscape of the interior. Equally alluring is the coastline of dramatic sea cliffs and headlands. Neighbouring Santa Maria has the Azores' warmest climate, where sunshine nourishes vineyards and pastures, and illuminates sandy bays.

The scenic São Miguel island

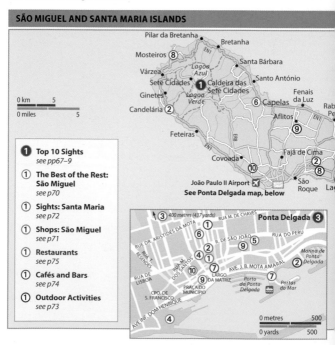

SÃO MIGUEL AND SANTA MARIA ISLANDS

① **Top 10 Sights**
see pp67–9

① **The Best of the Rest: São Miguel**
see p70

① **Sights: Santa Maria**
see p72

① **Shops: São Miguel**
see p71

① **Restaurants**
see p75

① **Cafés and Bars**
see p74

① **Outdoor Activities**
see p73

1 Caldeira das Sete Cidades
MAP A5 ■ São Miguel

According to local lore, a blue-eyed shepherd boy once fell for a green-eyed princess, but it was a forbidden romance. The pair parted, shedding tears that formed Lagoa Azul and Lagoa Verde – the blue and green lakes sunk into this volcanic crater (see pp14–15). From the Vista do Rei lookout, the crater reveals itself, its rim rising to nearly 300 m (1,000 ft) above the water's surface in places.

The historic city of Ponta Delgada

2 Ribeira Grande
MAP C5 ■ São Miguel

A sweeping beach, Praia de Santa Bárbara, fronts the island's second-largest town. The historic centre has gems such as Igreja da Misericórdia, with its Baroque façade, and Ponte dos Oito Arcos, the bridge of eight arches – a 19th-century landmark. The nearby Arquipélago – Centro de Artes Contemporâneas is an example of daring 21st-century design.

3 Ponta Delgada
MAP B6 ■ São Miguel

Narrow cobbled lanes, leafy squares and pretty parks characterize the Azores' busiest town (see pp12–13). Splendid palaces, Baroque mansions and impressive 16th-century churches and convents enhance the historic urban makeup. The 18th-century Portas da Cidade reflect the town's maritime heritage. An esplanade links the Renaissance Forte de São Brás at the harbour's western end with the modern Portas do Mar to the east.

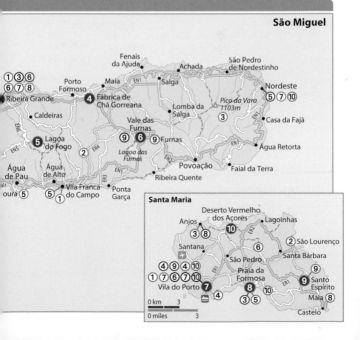

4 Fábrica de Chá Gorreana

MAP D5 ■ Plantações de Chá Gorreana, São Miguel ■ (296) 442 349 ■ Open 8am–6pm Mon–Fri, 9am–6pm Sat & Sun

Founded in 1883, the Gorreana tea estate is the only one of its kind left in Europe. Terraces of bushes on hills surround the *fábrica* (factory). The organic shoot tips, hand-picked from April to September, are processed using original machinery dating back to 1840. Teas can be bought in the showroom.

Tea plantations at Gorreana estate

5 Lagoa do Fogo

MAP D5 ■ São Miguel

Located within a nature reserve, the expansive "fire lake" is at the bottom of an ancient caldera on Água de Pau Massif. Clinging to its walls is a dense blanket of vegetation. Birdlife flourishes here: Atlantic yellow-legged gulls can be spotted gliding over the crater's lip. The Pico da Barrosa overlook offers the best views.

6 Vale das Furnas

The Furnas Valley *(see pp18–19)* meanders over a geothermal landscape of hot springs. On the northern shores of Lagoa das Furnas the volcanic ground is so hot that islanders come here to cook *cozido*, burying the pots in the earth for several hours *(see p55)*. The village of Furnas, surrounded by fumaroles, squats in a huge caldera. The verdant, perfumed 18th-century Parque Terra Nostra is laid out here, textured by trees and plants such as hibiscus and rhododendron. Visitors can bathe in the warm therapeutic waters of the park's swimming pool.

7 Vila do Porto

MAP E2 ■ Santa Maria

Unassuming Porto became Vila do Porto after receiving its charter in 1470, the first town in the Azores elevated to such a status. There is little left of Santa Maria's 15th-century capital, save for some weathered façades that would once have turned heads. Still spruce is the 16th-century Forte de São Brás. The engaging Centro de Interpretação Ambiental Dalberto Pombo *(see p72)* houses the personal collection of local naturalist Dalberto Pombo, a pioneer in the study of the island's natural heritage.

8 Praia da Formosa

MAP E2 ■ Santa Maria

One of the most popular beaches of the archipelago, Praia da Formosa is hemmed in by steep cliffs, with fields and meadows forming a pleasing

The inky-blue Lagoa do Fogo

GONÇALO VELHO CABRAL

Credited with the discovery in 1431 of the Ilhéus das Formigas, scattered islets in the Eastern Group of islands, Portuguese explorer Gonçalo Velho Cabral (c.1400–1460) later rediscovered Santa Maria and São Miguel islands. He was appointed Capitão Donatário (lord proprietor) of both islands, the first to hold the newly created title.

pastoral backdrop. The half-moon beach of white sand sits in one of the loveliest corners of the island. As an exposed beach and reef break, this is an internationally renowned surf spot; an area is marked off for surfers. Amenities include changing facilities and showers, and a handy bar-café.

9 Santo Espírito
MAP F2 ■ Santa Maria

There are two good reasons to explore this limewashed village: first, the pretty Igreja de Nossa Senhora da Purificação (see p38), and secondly, the Cooperativa de Artesanato de Santa Maria (see p58), a handicrafts cooperative with its own bakery. The homemade bread and biscoitos de orelha are irresistible, and the home-spun blankets make ideal souvenirs.

10 Deserto Vermelho dos Açores
MAP E2 ■ Santa Maria

One of the most surprising natural phenomena of the archipelago is the "Red Desert of the Azores" (see p43). This wave-like landscape near Santa Maria's northern shores is referred to as Barreiro da Faneca in Portuguese. It is an arid blanket of Pliocene sediments composed of clay minerals spread over ancient lava flow from Pico Alto, the island's highest point. Covered by pyroclasts (volcanic fragments), the clay oxidized to produce an environment akin to that of Mars.

EXPLORING SANTA MARIA ISLAND

▶ MORNING

Start the day with coffee and torrada (toast) at **Garrouchada** (see p74) in **Vila do Porto**. Drive north to ER-1-2 and then turn east to Almagreira. From here it is a short drive south to **Praia** where a glorious beach frames the shallow bay. Dip your toes in the crystalline water before returning to Almagreira. Continue east to **Santo Espírito**. Spend time here admiring the **Igreja de Nossa Senhora da Purificação** (see p38) and then browse the handicrafts at the **Cooperativa de Artesanato de Santa Maria** (see p58). Don't forget to try their homemade biscuits (see p59). If you have some time, nip into the nearby **Museu de Santa Maria** (see p72). The scenic ER-3-2 eventually brings you to **Baía de São Lourenço** (see p72). Stop for lunch at one of the cafés lining the beachfront.

AFTERNOON

Suitably refreshed, change gear and take ER-2-2 towards Santa Bárbara. This is one of the prettiest drives on the island. After skirting the coast near Lagoinhos the road snakes inland towards São Pedro. Carry on for 10 minutes and then take a right towards Anjos. This village is known for the historic **Capela de Nossa Senhora dos Anjos** (see p39) and its association with Christopher Columbus. Later, double back through Pedras de São Pedro. Relive the day over drinks at the **Central Pub** (see p74) in **Vila do Porto**.

See map on pp66–7 ←

The Best of the Rest: São Miguel

1 Vila Franca do Campo
MAP D6 ■ Ilhéu de Vila Franca
■ Ferries: Jun–Sep ■ Adm

A timeless air pervades this appealing coastal village. Out to sea is Ilhéu de Vila Franca, the remains of an old volcano. This islet hosts the Red Bull cliff-diving competition (see p63).

2 Lagoa do Congro
MAP D6

This lagoon is spellbinding for its ethereal beauty. Reached via a forest trail, the lake's surface resembles a pea-green oval mirror.

3 Serra da Tronqueira
MAP F5 ■ Centro Ambiental do Priolo: Reserva Forestal da Cancela do Cinzeiro ■ www.centropriolo.com

The wooded Tronqueira hill range is home to the rare Azores bullfinch (see p52). A visitor centre explains more.

4 Museu Militar dos Açores
MAP U2 ■ Forte de São Brás, Avenida Infante Dom Henrique, Ponta Delgada
■ (296) 308 633 ■ Adm

Examine historical armaments such as the rare palm-sized German Mauser pistol. The 16th-century fort can also be explored.

5 Caloura
MAP C6

This fishing village is highly regarded for its seafood restaurants (see p75). The natural harbour-side swimming pools provide endless fun, while the 16th-century private chapel and convent can be admired from afar.

6 Oficina-Museu das Capelas
MAP B5 ■ Rua do Loural 56, Capelas
■ (296) 298 202 ■ Closed Sun ■ Adm

Local resident Manuel João Melo built this museum as a 1940s-era street lined with shops and a bar, recreated using period furniture and fittings.

Cannon, Museu Militar dos Açores

Miradouro da Ponta do Arnel

7 Nordeste
MAP F5

Explore the eastern tip of the island and Serra da Tronqueira from this town. The lookout, Miradouro da Ponta do Arnel, peers over a craggy headland topped by a lighthouse.

8 Arquipélago-Centro de Artes Contemporâneas
MAP C5 ■ Rua Adolfo Coutinho de Medeiros, Ribeira Grande ■ Adm
■ www.arquipelagocentro deartes.azores. gov.pt

This former tobacco factory has been transformed into a premier visual and performing arts venue, with an exhibition space, a high-tech stage and a multimedia centre.

9 Torre Sineira
MAP U2 ■ Rua do Açoreano Oriental, Ponta Delgada ■ Closed Sat & Sun

The bell tower houses a massive 16th-century bronze bell, the oldest in Azores. Rooftop offers fine views.

10 Sinagoga de Ponta Delgada
MAP U2 ■ Rua do Brum 14–16, Ponta Delgada ■ Closed Sat & Sun

The 19th-century Sahar Hassamain (Gates of Heaven) Synagogue is the oldest in Portugal. It retains its ark, benches, bimah and wall panelling.

Shops: São Miguel

① Louvre Michaelense
MAP U2 ■ Rua António José D'Almeida 8, Ponta Delgada ■ (938) 346 886

Head here *(see p59)* for hand-stitched soft toy whales and delightful green tea and cake.

② Quintal dos Açores
MAP A5 ■ Rua da Canadinha 20a, Candelária ■ www.quintaldos acores.com

This family business produces jellies, jams, honey, pickles and sauces handmade to traditional recipes.

③ Parque Atlântico
MAP U1 ■ Rua da Juventude, Ponta Delgada ■ www.parque atlanticoshopping.pt

A supermarket anchors retail outlets, restaurants, cafés and a multiplex cinema to this shopping mall *(see p58)*.

④ Paulo do Vale
MAP U2 ■ Rua Machado dos Santos 89/91, Ponta Delgada ■ www.paulodovale.com

Skilled goldsmith Paulo do Vale fashions exquisite jewellery from gold, silver and Azorean black lava stone.

⑤ Mercado da Graça
MAP V2 ■ Rua do Mercado 15, Ponta Delgada

A rich bounty of local produce, such as *annonas* (custard apples) and *inhame das furnas* (yam from Furnas) graces the island's biggest market.

Local produce at Mercado da Graça

⑥ Fábrica de Licores Mulher de Capote
MAP C5 ■ Rua do Berquó 12, Ribeira Grande ■ www.mulherdecapote.pt

The liqueurs for sale at this distillery can be sampled as part of a free guided tour of the facility.

⑦ Liberty Store
MAP C5 ■ Avenida Dr José Nunes da Ponte, Ribeira Grande ■ www.island-import.com

Branded imported goods ranging from Maine blueberry muffins to Carolina's American Candies are on offer here.

Pottery on display at Cerâmica Vieira

⑧ Cerâmica Vieira
MAP A6 ■ Rua das Alminhas 10/12, Lagoa ■ (296) 912 116 ■ Closed Sat pm & Sun

Admire ceramic products at this factory *(see p58)* with a showroom, in business since 1862.

⑨ Com Certeza Gourmet
MAP V2 ■ Rua Dr Francisco Machado Fario e Maia 22, Ponta Delgada ■ www.comcerteza.pt

The range of Portuguese wines at this deli is impressive. Condiments include *flor de sal* (sea salt).

⑩ Posto de Turismo-Nordeste
MAP F5 ■ Rua António Alves de Oliveira, Nordeste ■ (296) 488 320

This tourist office also sells handicrafts such as cornhusk dolls and hand-embroidered tablecloths *(see p61)*.

See map on pp66–7 ←

Sights: Santa Maria

1 Forte de São Brás
MAP E2 ■ EN1-2A, Vila do Porto

Perched on a bluff overlooking the harbour, this well-preserved 16th-century stronghold houses the chapel of Nossa Senhora da Conceição. Admire the fine sea views from here.

A village along Baía de São Lourenço

2 Baía de São Lourenço
MAP F2 ■ São Lourenço

The terraced vineyards on the steep cliffs rearing up from São Lourenço Bay add texture to the dramatic perspective. The unique landscape is a protected nature reserve.

3 Capela de Nossa Senhora dos Anjos
MAP D1 ■ Anjos

Crew members from the *Niña*, a caravel commanded by Christopher Columbus, are believed to have prayed here *(see p39)* in 1493 during the voyage home from the Americas.

4 Pedreira do Campo
MAP E2 ■ Pico do Facho

A 100-m (328-ft) wall of pillow lava looms over a rich vein of exposed sediments and oceanic fossils, estimated to be five million years old.

5 Praia
MAP E2

Popular with watersports enthusiasts who are drawn to its shallow bay and the sandy Praia da Formosa *(see pp68–9)*, the village was once guarded from pirates by the long ruined 17th-century Forte de São João Baptista.

6 Pico Alto
MAP E2

At 590 m (1,935 ft), the summit of Santa Maria's highest peak is a tempting proposition for hikers. There is also a poignant reminder of a 1989 plane crash, marked by a memorial.

7 Centro de Interpretação Ambiental Dalberto Pombo
MAP E2 ■ Rua Teófilo Braga 10–14, Vila do Porto ■ (296) 206 798 ■ Open 9am–12:30pm & 1:30–5pm daily; closed Oct–Apr: Sat & Sun ■ Adm

The Casa dos Fósseis adds an exciting dimension to this excellent environmental interpretation centre.

8 Maia
MAP F2

The near-vertical stone terracing for grapevines on cliffs near Maia's Farol de Gonçalo Velho, a 1920s lighthouse, almost defies gravity. The wine, *vinho da cheiro*, is a popular local tipple.

9 Museu de Santa Maria
MAP F2 ■ Rua do Museu, Santo Espírito ■ (296) 884 844 ■ Open Apr–Sep: 10am–5:30pm Tue–Sun; Oct–Mar: 9:30am–5pm Tue–Sun ■ Adm

This delightful ethnographic museum displays local curios and antique hand-me-downs. The kitchen earthenware and period costumes stand out.

10 Ribeira de Maloás
MAP E2 ■ Barreiro da Malbusca

After prolonged rainfall, the bubbling stream trickling over the lip of this enormous basalt column formation becomes a picturesque waterfall.

Outdoor Activities

1 **Bird-Watching**
Gerby Birding:
www.gerbybirding.com
The rare Azores bullfinch is
the one to watch on São
Miguel. It is worth taking
a trip to the other island
for spotting the equally
elusive Santa Maria
goldcrest *(see pp52–3)*.

Azores bullfinch

2 **Whale Watching**
MAP V2 ■ Futurismo:
www.futurismo.pt
Encounters with these majestic
mammals are mesmerizing. Several
species can be seen throughout the
year. Lively dolphins always make the
occasions high-spirited *(see pp16–17)*.

3 **Surfing**
MAP C5 ■ Azores Surf Center:
www.azoressurfcenter.com
Two beaches on São Miguel stand
out: Areais de Santa Bárbara, on the
north coast, and Milícias near Ponta
Delgada. Santa Maria is home to
the Anjos and Formosa beaches.

4 **Walking**
Azores Trails of Nature:
www.azorestrailsofnature.com
Walking tours are a treat for the
senses. Tread a path across an
astonishing variety of landscapes –
lush pastureland, cratered hills,
barren sands and coastal plains.

5 **Cycling**
Azores MTB: www.azores
mtb.com
Pedal off-road for all-mountain rides
and a pure adrenaline rush. The
quiet rural lanes of the islands are
also ideal for exploring on bikes.

6 **Canyoning**
MAP E2 ■ Bootlá – Natureza &
Aventura: www.bootla.pt
Rappel narrow canyons under
waterfalls and into hidden lakes. Be
prepared to climb, scramble, swim
and jump to reach your destination.

7 **Diving**
MAP E2 ■ Mantamaria
Dive Center: www.divecenter.manta
maria.com
São Miguel and Santa Maria
benefit from their proximity
to the Dollabarat seamount
and Ilhéus das Formigas,
two marine reserves
teeming with dusky
grouper, box ray and
amberjack, among other
fish *(see pp24–5)*.

8 **Horse Riding**
MAP C6 ■ Equitur: www.
equitur.pt
Exploring on horseback takes
riders off the beaten track –
follow scenic bridleways astride
a purebred Lusitano to see the
Azorean landscape.

9 **Golfing**
MAP E5 ■ Azores Golf Islands:
www.azoresgolfislands.com
Tee off in the mid-Atlantic at the
Batalha golf course, which affords
sweeping ocean views. A luxuriant
volcanic landscape wraps itself
around the Furnas course.

The verdant Batalha golf course

10 **Sailing**
MAP E2 ■ Goldensail: www.
goldensailazores.com
Seasoned yachties who have the
necessary certification can charter
a boat and navigate between the two
islands. Landlubbers can choose a
themed tour captained by a skipper.

See map on pp66–7 ←

Cafés and Bars

1 **3/4 Café**
MAP U1 ■ Rua Dr Guilherme Poças Falcão 10, Ponta Delgada, São Miguel ■ (915) 088 070 ■ Closed Mon & Sun

Soups, hamburgers and homemade cakes form the menu here (see p57). Nightfall brings a free-spirited crowd.

Outdoor seating at Mascote

2 **The Gin Library**
MAP B6 ■ Solar Branco Eco Estate, Livramento, Ponta Delgada, São Miguel ■ (919) 076 779 ■ Open 4:30–7pm Tue–Sun

Sample Europe's largest collection of gin – over 600 gins from more than 34 countries – either in the library itself or in Senhor Raposa's Secret Drinking Den (see p57).

3 **Paquete**
MAP E2 ■ Praia Formosa, Santa Maria ■ (296) 884 142

This popular seafront restaurant lies opposite the Beach Parque leisure facility (open Jun–Sep).

4 **Central Pub**
MAP E2 ■ Rua Dr Luís Bettencourt 20, Vila do Porto, Santa Maria ■ (296) 882 513

This jolly American-style pub is all about relaxing with ice-cold beer.

5 **O Forno**
MAP F5 ■ Rua Dona Maria do Rosario, Nordeste, São Miguel ■ (296) 488 200

Breakfasts, snacks and light meals are available at this homely establishment. The hot bread rolls are served straight from the *forno* (oven).

6 **TukáTulá Bar**
MAP C5 ■ Areal de Santa Bárbara, Ribeira Grande, São Miguel ■ (296) 477 647

A favourite hang-out for surfers, this bar-restaurant is popular for its savvy design and stunning views.

7 **Mascote**
MAP V2 ■ Largo da Matriz 62, Ponta Delgada, São Miguel ■ (296) 284 399 ■ Closed Sun

Close to the Igreja Matriz de São Sebasião, this friendly café is popular with locals. It offers a good-value menu with delectable seafood dishes.

8 **Bar dos Anjos**
MAP D1 ■ Lugar dos Anjos, Anjos, Santa Maria ■ (296) 886 260 ■ Closed Mon

The "angel's bar" is situated over a terraced pool complex built around natural rock pools. Crowded and animated during the day, evening brings sundowners and a lighter vibe.

9 **Garrouchada**
MAP E2 ■ Rua Dr Luís Bettencourt 25, Vila do Porto, Santa Maria ■ (296) 883 038

Unwind on the pleasant terrace over morning coffee and cake, or drop by later for a delectable seafood platter. Dinner here is a hearty affair. Book ahead during the summer season.

10 **Lava Jazz Bar**
MAP B6 ■ Avenida Roberto Ivens, Ponta Delgada, São Miguel ■ (917) 350 418

The toe-tapping jazz at this elegant venue ups Ponta Delgada's nightlife tempo. National line-ups and invited musicians from overseas deliver sets layered with multitextured rhythms.

Restaurants

1 Alabote
MAP C5 ■ Rua East Providence 68, Ribeira Grande, São Miguel ■ (296) 473 516 ■ Closed Wed ■ €€

Alabote has garnered praise for its creative take on traditional cuisine.

2 Alcides
MAP U2 ■ Rua Hintze Ribeiro 67, Ponta Delgada, São Miguel ■ (296) 629 884 ■ Closed Sun ■ €€

Celebrated for its steaks, the kitchen is also noted for its seafood (see p57).

3 Caloura Bar-Esplanade
MAP C6 ■ Porta da Caloura, São Miguel ■ (296) 913 283 ■ €€

Crashing waves, cackling gulls and the tang of grilled fish set the scene here.

4 Mesa d'Oito
MAP E2 ■ Rua Teófilo de Braga 31, Vila do Porto, Santa Maria ■ (296) 882 083 ■ Closed Mon ■ €€

Diners at the Charming Blue Hotel can enjoy a short but satisfying menu.

5 Atlântico
MAP D6 ■ Rua Vasco da Silveira 10, Vila Franca do Campo, São Miguel ■ (296) 583 360 ■ Closed Mon ■ €€

Tables on the terrace offer romantic views of Ilhéu de Vila Franca (see p70).

6 Rotas da Ilha Verde
MAP U2 ■ Rua Pedro Homem 49, Ponta Delgada, São Miguel ■ (296) 628 560 ■ Closed Mon & Sun ■ €€

Scuffed tabletops and odd chairs give this vegetarian restaurant an appealingly disorganized vibe (see p56). Expect tofu, quinoa and other healthy items.

PRICE CATEGORIES

For a three-course meal for one with half a bottle of wine (or equivalent meal), taxes and extra charges.

€ under €20   €€ €20–40   €€€ over €40

Sophisticated interior of Anfiteatro

7 Anfiteatro
MAP V2 ■ Portas do Mar, Ponta Delgada, São Miguel ■ (296) 206 154 ■ €€€

Reinvented island cuisine and local wine pairing match the stylish, minimalist decor (see p56).

8 Gázcidla
MAP A4 ■ Rua da Ponte 16, Mosteiros, São Miguel ■ (296) 915 469 ■ Closed Mon ■ €

Come here for *polvo assado* – roasted octopus drizzled with red wine sauce.

9 Tony's
MAP E5 ■ Largo da Teatro 5, Furnas, São Miguel ■ (296) 584 290 ■ €€

Tony's dishes up the stew cooked underground near Furnas lake – *cozido das Furnas (see p55)*. It is popular, so book ahead.

10 DuFogo
MAP E2 ■ Rua da Olivença 11, Vila do Porto, Santa Maria ■ (296) 882 000 ■ Closed Sun ■ €

Eat in or takeaway from a great choice of steaks and grilled skewers.

Cloth menu at Rotas da Ilha Verde

See map on pp66–7 ←

TOP 10 Terceira and Graciosa Islands

Deriving its name from the fact that it was the third island to be discovered, Terceira is home to the most beautiful town in the Azores: Angra do Heroísmo. The historic island's interior impresses with an ancient volcanic landscape of plunging caves, mysterious cones and sweeping massifs. Try the wines cultivated from black, serrated lava plains and look out for the island-wide *impérios* – the dainty chapels of the Holy Spirit – that are some of the most ornate in the archipelago. Peppered with scarlet-topped windmills, the rural idyll that is Graciosa, the Azores' second smallest island, has a pleasant yesteryear appeal. Renowned for its historic natural spa facilities, terraced vineyards that cling precariously to forbidding sea cliffs and a volcanic cavern set deep underground, the entire island is a UNESCO designated Biosphere Reserve.

Obelisk at Angra do Heroísmo

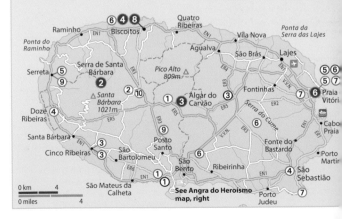

TERCEIRA AND GRACIOSA ISLANDS

① **Top 10 Sights**
see pp77–9

① **The Best of the Rest: Terceira**
see p80

① **Attractions: Graciosa**
see p81

① **Shops**
see p82

① **Restaurants**
see p85

① **Cafés and Bars**
see p84

① **Outdoor Activities**
see p83

Terceir

Raminho · Biscoitos · Quatro Ribeiras · Vila Nova · Ponta da Serra das Lajes

Ponta do Raminho

Serreta · Serra de Santa Bárbara · Pico Alto 809m · Águalva · São Brás · Lajes

Santa Bárbara 1021m · Algar do Carvão · Fontinhas · Praia Vitóri

Doze Ribeiras · Cabo Praia

Santa Bárbara · Posto Santo · Serra do Cume · Fonte do Bastardo · Porto Martir

Cinco Ribeiras · São Bartolomeu · São Bento · Ribeirinha · São Sebastião

São Mateus da Calheta · **See Angra do Heroísmo map, right** · Porto Judeu

0 km 4
0 miles 4

1 Angra do Heroísmo

Exploring this Terceira town *(see pp20–21)* – a UNESCO World Heritage Site – is an enchanting experience. There is a remarkable portfolio of historic property, including churches, convents and balconied palaces, all in pristine condition. Visit Angra do Heroísmo to see not one but many towns, shaped over centuries by European, American and Asian cultural influences.

2 Serra de Santa Bárbara

MAP L5 ■ Centro de Interpretação da Serra de Santa Bárbara, Estrada das Doze, Terceira ■ (295) 403 957 ■ Open 9am– 12:30pm & 1:30–5pm daily; closed Oct–Apr: Sat & Sun ■ Adm

The Santa Bárbara hill range presents visitors with a landscape brushed by heather and juniper. On the summit is a protected nature reserve that hugs a crater – at 1,021 m (3,350 ft)

this is the island's highest point. The views beyond embrace other islands in the Central Group, anchored in a blue Atlantic. The interpretation centre provides background information.

3 Algar do Carvão

Daylight diminishes as visitors descend this volcanic chimney *(see pp30–31)* on Terceira, an astonishing natural phenomenon. The result of an eruption about 2,000 years ago, the vent plunges 100 m (328 ft) below the surface to widen into a series of huge caverns. The conduit drops further and ends in a lake fed by rainwater. A Regional Natural Monument, the lava tube is near the Caldeira Guilherme Moniz.

Museu do Vinho dos Biscoitos

4 Museu do Vinho dos Biscoitos

MAP M4 ■ Canada do Caldeiro, nr Biscoitos, Terceira ■ (965) 667 324 ■ Open May–Sep: 10am–5:30pm Tue– Sun; Oct–Apr: 1:30–4pm Tue–Sat

The Biscoitos winery is renowned for its Verdelho wines – labels such as Da Resistência – and the fortified liqueurs Vinho Generoso and Chico Maria. Custodian of the on-site museum Luís Brum imparts the history behind the antique artifacts used in the cultivation and picking of grapes. The vineyard tour includes wine tasting.

5 Furna do Enxofre

MAP K6 ■ Centro de Visitantes da Furna do Enxofre, Caldeira da Graciosa, Graciosa ■ (295) 714 009 ■ Open 9am–12:30pm & 1:30–5pm daily; closed Oct–Apr: Mon ■ Adm

Of great speleological importance, this volcanic cave *(see p42)* is one of the most significant geosites in the Azores. Set under the island's caldera, it is 194 m (636 ft) wide and reaches 50 m (164 ft) high in places. The cavern features a convex ceiling with stalactites and mineral deposits, and the floor cups a fumarole. A lake occupies the deepest part of the cave, the floor of which lies below sea level. There is an interpretative centre and guided tours are offered.

Furna do Enxofre volcanic cave

6 Praia da Vitória

MAP P5 ■ Terceira

A wedge of pale sand and a busy marina lend this port a holiday-resort atmosphere. Terceira's second-largest town was once known as Vila da Praia, but after the Liberal forces overran the Absolutists here in 1829 *(see pp36–7)*, it was renamed Praia da Vitória to commemorate the victory. The pedestrianized streets leading off the main square, Praça Francisco Ornelas da Câmara, make for rewarding shopping, and some of the archipelago's more elaborate *impérios* are found nearby.

Fishermen's Monument, Praia da Vitória

7 Santa Cruz da Graciosa

MAP J5 ■ Graciosa

Dotted with church spires and, on its outskirts, red-topped basalt windmills, Graciosa's main town exudes a bygone charm. Incongruous against this traditional setting is the modern wing of the Museu da Graciosa *(see p41)*. The island's viticulture tradition is upheld at the Pedras Brancas winery. A grand perspective of the area can be had from Monte da Ajuda *(see p81)*.

8 Biscoitos

MAP M4 ■ Terceira

A coastal area synonymous with Verdelho wines, this region is named for the nuggets of solidified black lava deposited after an eruption in 1761 – the oval shapes reminded early settlers of their boat bread, or *biscoito* (biscuit), supply. Wine has been produced here since the 16th century, cultivated from vineyards pocketed within walled enclosures called *curraletas*. It is an intriguing landscape made even more attractive by the enticing natural rock pools *(see p44)* near the harbour.

9 Ilhéu da Praia

MAP K5 ■ Graciosa

Poking out of the water 1 km (half a mile) off the coast of Praia, this tiny basalt islet is home to a variety of sea-birds, the Azores'

Santa Cruz da Graciosa viewed from Monte de Ajuda

most diverse colony. A Special Protected Area indicative of Graciosa's UNESCO Biosphere Reserve classification, the ocean-lapped rock attracts many migratory species but the one bird every ornithologist trains their binoculars on is the Monteiro's storm petrel *(see p52)*.

⑩ Termas do Carapacho

MAP K6 ■ Rua Dr Manuel de Sousa Menezes, Carapacho, Graciosa ■ (295) 714 212 ■ Open Jul–Sep: 9am– 7pm Tue–Sun; Oct–Jun: noon–7pm Tue–Fri, 10am–5pm Sat & Sun ■ Adm

Musculoskeletal and dermatological disorders are treated here using the island's curative geothermal water; the spa also offers a menu that includes float therapy and Vichy showers. After an indulgent soak, pamper yourself with a sleep-inducing massage. There has been a spa on this site since 1750 and the foundations of the original building can still be seen.

THE 1980 EARTHQUAKE

On 1 January 1980 an earthquake measuring 7.2 on the Richter scale struck the Azores. The tremor shook the Central Group of islands, and Terceira bore the brunt. Angra's historic quarter suffered damage but it was Doze Ribeiras *(see p80)*, the village nearest the epicentre, that was worst affected. In all, 61 people perished while 15,000 were made homeless.

▶ MORNING

Start your exploration of this fascinating UNESCO World Heritage Site with breakfast at **Verde Maçã Café** *(see p84)* on Rua Direita. Afterwards, walk to **Palácio dos Capitães Generais** *(see p20)*, the former residence of the island's governor, and join a guided tour of the palace. Next, wander through the **Jardim Duque da Terceira** *(see p21)*, one of the most attractive public gardens in the Azores, and climb the steps to **Outeiro da Memória** *(see p21)*, or Memorial Hill. On a sunny day the panorama over the town is quite uplifting. Retrace your route to the **Convento de São Francisco**, which houses Angra's excellent museum *(see p40)*. Spend an hour here admiring the different collections that illustrate the island's history. Amble back towards Rua de São João for a hearty meal at **O Chico** *(see p85)*.

AFTERNOON

Start the afternoon by visiting the impressive 18th-century **Igreja da Misericórdia** *(see p38)*, its pale blue façade a familiar harbourfront landmark. Stroll along the quayside before heading back into the historic centre. Pick up Rua da Rosa to make your way to the ornate 16th-century **Convento de São Gonçalo** *(see p39)*. From here it is a short jaunt west to **Fortaleza de São João Baptista** *(see p21)*. Tread the weathered battlements and if you are fortunate, a late-afternoon sun will burnish the views with gold.

See map on pp76–7 ←

The Best of the Rest: Terceira

1 Circuito das Furnas de Enxofre
MAP M5

An interesting diversion, the trail snakes over fumaroles and hot springs. The information panels explain more about the landscape (see p31).

2 Mistérios Negros
MAP M5

The "dark mysteries" are trachyte rock domes bereft of vegetation. Admire these volcanic phenomena on the walk from the Gruta do Natal visitor centre near Lagoa do Negro.

3 Cinco Ribeiras
MAP L5

This pretty village is known for its delicious *vaquinha* cheese (see p83), scenic harbour and the swimming facilities at Ponta das Cinco Ribeiras.

4 Doze Ribeiras
MAP L5

Every year the houses in this village are repainted to herald the Holy Ghost festivities (see p62). This act also marks the 1980 earthquake (see p79).

5 Império da Caridade
MAP P5 ▪ Rua do Cruzeiro, Praia da Vitória ▪ Closed to the public

The *impérios* (empires) of the Holy Spirit (see p62) are chapel-like structures seen across the Azores. They are especially ornate on Terceira, which has about 70 *impérios*.

6 Serra do Cume
MAP N5 ▪ Miradouro da Serra do Cume

At 545 m (1,788 ft), Serra do Cume's highest point offers a splendid view of Praia da Vitória, but it is the stone-walled fields that eyes are drawn to.

7 Ponta das Contendas
MAP P6

The islets around the Contendas promontory harbour seabirds. Nearby, São Sebastião commemorates the 1581 Battle of Salga with a monument.

8 Os Montanheiros
MAP U4

All kinds of information about the Azores' volcanic caves can be found at the Society of Exploration and Speleology headquarters (see p30).

9 Serreta
MAP L5

Explore the village and lighthouse as part of a stroll to Ponta do Raminho. In summer the cliffs come alive with nesting Cory's shearwaters (see p53).

10 Gruta do Natal
MAP M5 ▪ Pico Gordo, Reserva Florestal Natural da Serra de Santa Bárbara ▪ Open Apr–Sep: pm daily; closed Oct–Mar: Mon, Thu & Sun ▪ Adm ▪ www.montanheiros.com

This circular lava tube is well signed with explanations that identify the lava formations.

The bright, colourful façade of the Império da Caridade

Attractions: Graciosa

(1) Adega e Cooperativa Agrícola da Ilha Graciosa

MAP J5 ∎ Charco da Cruz 12, Santa Cruz da Graciosa ∎ (295) 712 169 ∎ Open 9am–5pm Mon–Fri

Tour the winery (see p59) before uncorking the wines, such as the flagship VQPRD Pedras Brancas, a white with fresh fruit notes.

(2) Moinhos de Vento

MAP K5

Early Flemish settlers left these basalt stone windmills with red cupolas. Many have wooden latticed spokes, sometimes with sails.

Flemish windmill with red cupola, Graciosa

(3) Monte da Ajuda

MAP K5

From this lofty vantage point Santa Cruz da Graciosa resembles a picture postcard. Three chapels, including the Ermida da Nossa Senhora da Ajuda (see p39), occupy the summit.

(4) Museu da Graciosa

MAP K5 ∎ Largo Conde de Simas 17, Santa Cruz da Graciosa ∎ Open Apr–Sep: 10am–5:30pm Tue–Sun, Oct–Mar: 9:30am–5:30pm Tue–Sun ∎ (295) 712 429 ∎ Adm

This museum (see p41) houses local artifacts and curios. Exhibits include a miller's horse-driven grinding stone.

(5) Praia (São Mateus)

MAP K5

Fishing is the main economic activity of this attractive port. The praia (beach) nets summertime crowds.

(6) Casa Museu João Tomáz Bettencourt

MAP J5 ∎ Rua Eng. Marcelo Bettencourt 3, Guadalupe ∎ (295) 730 040 ∎ Open 8am–noon & 1–4pm Mon–Fri

This former 19th-century home and general store of a local trader is now a lovely museum.

(7) Associação de Criadores e Amigos do Burro Anão da Ilha Graciosa

MAP J5 ∎ Caminho da Esperança Velha 14, Ribeirinha ∎ (911) 001 936

The endangered Graciosa burro anão (dwarf donkey) is unique to the island. Franco Ceraolo runs a farm where visitors can get to know these animals.

(8) Associação de Artesãos da Ilha Graciosa

MAP J5 ∎ Rua Infante Dom Henrique 50, Santa Cruz da Graciosa ∎ (295) 712 837 ∎ Open 8:30am–12:30pm & 1:30–4:30pm Mon–Wed & Fri

This artisans' association (see p83) focuses on traditional embroidery.

Ilhéu da Baleia rock formation

(9) Ponta da Barca and Ilhéu da Baleia

MAP J4–5

At 23 m (75 ft), the Ponta da Barca lighthouse is the tallest in the Azores. Its tower looms over the headland and the "Whale Islet" rock formation.

(10) Tanque do – Atalho

MAP J5 ∎ Rua Engenheiro Manuel Rodrigues de Miranda, Santa Cruz da Graciosa ∎ Open 1:30–5pm Mon–Fri

This 1866-built underground vaulted cistern supplied water to Santa Cruz. Visitors descend via a steep stairwell.

See map on pp76–7

Outdoor Activities

1 **Diving**
MAP M6 ■ Espírito Azul: www.espiritoazul.com

The Banco Dom João de Castro seamount off Terceira is considered one of the archipelago's best dive sites (see p25). The Terceirense shipwreck is Graciosa's premier dive spot.

2 **Bird-Watching**
Gerby Birding: www.gerbybirding.com

Observe birdlife in their maritime habitats such as Ilhéu da Praia off Graciosa (see pp78–9). The Cabo da Praia and Ponta das Contendas (see p80) are Terceira's birding hot spots.

3 **Golf**
MAP N5 ■ Clube de Golfe da Ilha Terceira: www.terceiragolf.com

Several water features challenge accuracy of play on this 18-hole par-72 layout, considered the easiest of the islands' three courses.

4 **Whale and Dolphin Watching**
MAP V4 ■ Ocean Emotion: www.oceanemotion.pt

Whales can be spotted throughout the summer months, while several species of dolphins stay for winter. The sperm whale (see p17) is a notable year-round resident.

5 **Fishing**
Calypso Azores: www.calypsoazores.com

Whether trolling for sawfish, mackerel and barracuda, or bottom fishing from an anchored vessel to catch bream and snapper, the Azorean sea provides an amazing ocean bounty.

6 **Stand-up Paddleboarding (SUP)**
Vila Nova Surf Centre: www.vilanovasurf.com

Stand-up paddleboard over shallow waters and across spectacular bays while admiring the scenic coastline.

7 **Health and Wellbeing**
MAP K6 ■ Termas do Carapacho, Graciosa

Bathe in hot thermal waters, step under a Vichy shower or limber up in a hydrogymnastics class (see p79).

8 **Caving**
TuriAzores: www.turiazores.com

On Terceira, visitors can explore Algar do Carvão (see pp30–31). Graciosa lures with its striking Furna do Enxofre (see p78). Speleologists should visit Os Montanheiros (see p80).

9 **Horse Riding**
Quinta da Terça: www.quintadaterca.com

The Lusitano is an ideal horse breed on which to explore Terceira's forests. Youngsters will love the dwarf donkeys on Graciosa (see p81).

10 **Walking**
ComunicAir: www.comunicair.pt

The demanding 40-km (24-mile) circular Grande Rota da Graciosa takes in geosites such as Caldeirinha de Pêro Botelho. Terceira can be hiked using seven official trails.

Hiking on the hills of Terceira

Shops

1 QB Food Court
MAP M6 ■ Caminho do Meio de São Carlos 50, Angra do Heroísmo, Terceira ■ (295) 333 999

Buy artisan milk and dark chocolates as treats, or create your own gift box at this boutique café-restaurant.

Display window at O Forno

2 O Forno
MAP U4 ■ Rua de São João 67–69, Angra do Heroísmo, Terceira ■ (295) 213 729 ■ Closed Sun

O Forno is the place to indulge in Terceira's famed *bolos Dona Amélia*, sugar-coated cupcakes that are named after Portugal's last queen.

3 Queijo Vaquinha
MAP L5 ■ Canada Pilar 5, Cinco Ribeiras, Terceira ■ (295) 907 138

Take a guided tour of this cheese factory and sample their renowned *queijo vaquinha* (calf's cheese).

4 Mercado Duque de Bragança
MAP U3 ■ Rua da Sé, Angra do Heroísmo, Terceira ■ Closed Sat pm & Sun

This historic farmers' market is worth browsing for fresh fish and handpicked fruits and vegetables.

5 Bordado dos Açores
MAP U4 ■ Avenida José Agostinho 31, Angra do Heroísmo, Terceira ■ Closed from noon Sat & Sun

This long-established, family-run business *(see p58)* is noted for its hand-embroidered towels, curtains and tablemats, woven on site.

6 Quinta dos Açores
MAP N5 ■ Pico Redondo 149, São Bento, Terceira ■ (295) 216 213

Wines, fresh meat and dairy produce, assorted fruits and vegetables and homemade jams from across the islands are stocked at this impressive indoor deli-style market.

7 Casa Astória
MAP P5 ■ Rua de Jesus 103, Praia da Vitória, Terceira ■ (295) 512 945 ■ Closed Sat pm & Sun

Shop at Astória for traditional mementos such as plasterwork *impérios* – miniature replicas of the Holy Spirit chapels *(see p80)* found all over the islands and especially on Terceira.

8 Queijadas da Graciosa
MAP K5 ■ Queijadas da Graciosa 34–36, Rochela, Praia (São Mateus), Graciosa ■ (295) 712 911 ■ Closed Sun

The cinnamon-flavoured sweet and creamy cakelets are a regional delicacy. Take home a box or two.

9 Adega e Cooperativa Agrícola da Ilha Graciosa

Pedras Brancas wines including smooth Angelica Vinho Licoroso and fiery Aguardente Vínica are sold here *(see p81)*. Pink garlic and Galia melon produced in the same estate are also stocked.

10 Associação de Artesãos da Ilha Graciosa

Run by volunteers, the arts and crafts cooperative *(see p81)* of Graciosa is a joy to discover. The skilled women artisans create exquisitely embroidered tablecloths.

See map on pp76–7

Cafés and Bars

1 Verde Maçã Café
MAP V4 ■ Rua Direita 111–113, Angra do Heroísmo, Terceira ■ (295) 218 294 ■ Closed Sun

This bar-café is famous for its basalt stone arches and pop-art murals. The menu includes panini and bruschetta, alongside sinful desserts.

2 Pastelaria Athanasio
MAP U4 ■ Rua da Sé 132, Angra do Heroísmo, Terceira ■ (295) 218 470

A favourite with chocolate lovers, this historic bakery is known for their *cornucópias* (chocolate and custard cones). Try the *covilhete de leite*, a rich cinnamon cake.

3 Alto Sé Café
MAP M6 ■ Alto das Covas 1, Angra do Heroísmo, Terceira ■ (295) 707 700 ■ Closed Sun

Top spot for a milky coffee and a tasty pastry. It offers a great-value menu, which changes every day.

4 Birou Bar
MAP U4 ■ Rua de São João, Angra do Heroísmo, Terceira ■ (295) 702 180 ■ Closed Sun

Nip in here *(see p57)* for a frappé with whipped cream. Meals include Alentejana pork and tuna salad. The mojito is the cocktail of choice.

The interior of Birou Bar

5 Delman Bar & Lounge
MAP P5 ■ Avenida Marginal da Praia da Vitória 22A, Praia da Vitória, Terceira ■ (961) 836 423

Enjoy *petiscos* (snacks) at this lunchtime spot while admiring the pleasant waterfront view. The bar is known for its eye-popping gin menu.

6 Garça
MAP P5 ■ Avenida Álvaro Martins Homem, Praia da Vitória, Terceira ■ (295) 512 837

Patrons come to Garça, established in 1956, for good local cooking and a sports-pub atmosphere. There are occasional live-music performances.

7 Pub Bar Vila Sacramento
MAP J5 ■ Estrada Nova, Santa Cruz da Graciosa, Graciosa ■ (912) 063 872 ■ Open Fri & Sat

Expect a thumping mix of house, Latin and electro at this bar *(see p57)* and music club. Parties have previously featured African *kizomba* dancing.

8 Snack-Bar Jale
MAP J5 ■ Rua 25 de Abril 58–60, Santa Cruz da Graciosa, Graciosa ■ (295) 712 344

Tuck into delectable seafood dishes at this restaurant. House specials include *ameijoas de chefe con pão de alho* (chef's clams with garlic bread).

9 Café e Sabores Félix
MAP K5 ■ Rua Fontes Pereira de Melo 138, Praia, Graciosa ■ (295) 732 146

Drop by for some *queijadas da Graciosa* – cinnamon-flavoured star-shaped tarts filled with deliciously smooth caramel cream.

10 Grafil Coffee Bar
MAP J5 ■ Largo Conde de Simas 4, Santa Cruz da Graciosa, Graciosa ■ (295) 712 144

Sip a drink while watching innovative live-music sessions featuring rock and classically trained musicians.

Restaurants

① Cais de Angra
MAP V4 ■ Marina de Angra do Heroísmo, Terceira ■ (295) 628 458 ■ €€

Comfort food meets traditional Portuguese cuisine at this lively restaurant (see p56). Choose between gourmet burgers or dry-aged steaks. The *caipirinha* cocktails make perfect apéritifs.

② O Chico
MAP V4 ■ Rua de São João 7, Angra do Heroísmo, Terceira ■ (295) 333 286 ■ Closed Sun ■ €

Family run and exuding warmth and hospitality, O Chico is a favourite with locals. The menu lists Azorean staples including *alcatra* (see p54).

Simple setting at Remember Azores

③ Remember Azores
MAP K5 ■ Graciosa Resort, Porto da Barra, Graciosa ■ (919) 249 090 ■ €€

Azorean dishes, such as octopus, and grilled steak with cheese sauce, are served in a contemporary dining space.

④ Os Moínhos
MAP P6 ■ Rua do Arrabalde, São Sebastião, Terceira ■ (295) 904 508 ■ Closed Tue (in winter) ■ €€

Named for its ancient water wheel, this converted millhouse is the place to enjoy *telha de marisco*, a rich creamy casserole served in earthenware.

⑤ Ti Choa
MAP L5 ■ Groto do Margarida 1, Serreta, Terceira ■ (295) 906 673 ■ Closed Sun; Tue & Thu D ■ €

Dining in this rustic space (see p57) is like eating in a traditional farmhouse. The decor enhances the rural charm.

⑥ Casa de Pasto O Pedro
MAP M4 ■ Caminho do Concelho, Biscoitos, Terceira ■ (961) 434 988 ■ Closed Sun ■ €

The eclectic menu at this delightful restaurant features home-style dishes.

⑦ Casa de Pasto Bela Vista
MAP P5 ■ Vale Farto 30, nr Praia da Vitória, Terceira ■ (295) 513 424 ■ Closed Wed ■ €€

A stone-clad, country-style interior emphasizes the old-fashioned character of this good-value restaurant.

⑧ O Cachalote
MAP U3 ■ Rua do Rego 14, Angra do Heroísmo, Terceira ■ (914) 237 459 ■ Closed Sun; Mon–Sat L ■ €€

This hole-in-the-wall restaurant is known for its generous steaks.

⑨ Taberna Roberto
MAP M5 ■ Grota do Medo 1, Posta Santo, Angra do Heroísmo, Graciosa ■ (966) 431 126 ■ Closed Mon; Sun D ■ €€

The chef at this family-run restaurant serves hearty dishes, such as roasted pork, prepared in a wood-fired oven.

⑩ Dolphin Snack-Bar
MAP K6 ■ Caminho Carapacho, Carapacho, Graciosa ■ (295) 712 014 ■ €€

This spot is a short walk from the Carapacho Spa (see p79). Specialities are seafood dishes – try the octopus.

See map on pp76–7

🔟 São Jorge, Pico and Faial Islands

Resembling an emerald shard anchored in an ice-blue sea, São Jorge captivates with its superb hiking trails, many of which take in the famous *fajãs (see p43)*. The island's reputation extends to producing some of the tastiest cheeses in the Azores. Pico, dominated by its enormous volcanic cone, offers some of the world's most rewarding whale watching, while its vineyards are a UNESCO World Heritage Site. As the mid-Atlantic's yachting capital, nearby Faial is proud of its seafaring heritage. The central caldera astounds, but it is the Capelinhos volcano that truly captures the imagination.

Majestic Montanha do Pico

1 Montanha do Pico
MAP M3 ■ Casa da Montanha: Caminho Florestal 9, Pico ■ (967) 303 519

Portugal's highest mountain reaches 2,351 m (7,713 ft) above sea level and is emblematic of the Azores' natural wonders. It is possible to ascend Pico independently, but engaging an official guide is strongly

SÃO JORGE, PICO AND FAIAL ISLANDS

① **Top 10 Sights**
see pp88–91

① **The Best of the Rest: São Jorge**
see p92

① **Attractions: Pico**
see p93

① **Sights: Faial**
see p94

① **Restaurants**
see p97

① **Cafés and Bars**
see p96

① **Outdoor Activities**
see p95

Previous pages The striking façade of Império da Caridade in Praia da Vitória, Terceira

recommended. Alternatively, conquer the summit as part of a climbing group (see p95). The trailhead begins at the Casa da Montanha – the Mountain House – where climbers need to register.

2 Serra do Topo–Fajã da Caldeira de Santo Cristo–Fajã dos Cubres Trail

MAP Q2 ■ Centro de Interpretação da Fajã da Caldeira de Santo Cristo, São Jorge ■ (295) 403 860 ■ Open 9:30am–12:30pm & 1:30–4:30pm daily (Oct–May: Fri & Sat)

Serra do Topo is the departure point for one of the best walks in the Azores. Stunning views take in the Fajã da Caldeira de Santo Cristo lagoon. Once at Caldeira de Santo Cristo, visit the interpretation centre, which offers a fascinating glimpse into the geological and social history of the region. Find out more about the island's *fajãs* – classified by UNESCO as biosphere reserves – then continue towards the photogenic Fajã dos Cubres (see p43).

Rich decor of Igreja de Santa Bárbara

3 Igreja de Santa Bárbara

MAP N2 ■ Caminho de Baixa, Manadas, São Jorge ■ Closed Mon

This splendid 18th-century Baroque church (see p38) is one of the most richly decorated in the Azores, featuring panels of *azulejos* that illustrate the story of Santa Bárbara. The basalt-covered 16th-century font is the only surviving piece of the original church, while the excellent cedarwood ceiling is a rare architectural feature.

São Jorge, Pico and Faial Islands

4 Complexo Monte de Guia: Casa dos Dabney e Aquário de Porto Pim

Wealthy merchant John Bass Dabney (1766–1826) arrived here from Boston in 1804 and was soon appointed first US consul to the Azores. Whaling and other business interests generated wealth and prestige for the family, and the museum imparts their story. The pairing of the Casa dos Dabney (see p26) with the Aquário de Porto Pim (see p27) is convenient for visitors: the same ticket grants entry to the aquarium, which is a holding tank for various finned species who are later rehoused in aquariums around the world.

The brightly coloured Museu do Vinho

CABLE CAPITAL OF THE WORLD

Its mid-Atlantic position made Horta suitable for the anchoring of transatlantic telegraph cables. The first cable was laid in 1893, linking the town with Ponta Delgada and on to Carcavelos, near Lisbon. By the mid-20th century Horta was one of the world's most important cable centres, relaying messages and meteorological observations. The last cable company left in 1969.

5 Museu da Horta

Apart from displaying fig tree pith sculptures (see p61), Horta Museum records the island's artistic, nautical, technological and ethnographic development. The work of José Júlio de Sousa Pinto (1856–1939) is on display: look for his *A Volta dos Barcos* painting. A hall is dedicated to advancements in transatlantic telegraphic communications. The building was a Jesuit College; next door is the Igreja de São Salvador (see p27).

6 Museu do Vinho

Matchbox vineyards hemmed in by *currais* front this wine museum (see p32), which tells Pico's winemaking history through illustrated panels. Make sure you play the "Aromas" game, where you match different scents with various fruits and condiments. Later, discover a vintage winepress and other equipment. Finish up in the tasting room where wines can be sampled and purchased.

7 Gruta das Torres

MAP L2 ▪ Caminho da Gruta das Torres, Criação Velha, Pico ▪ (924) 403 921 ▪ Open May–Sep: 9am–12:30pm & 1:30–6pm daily (Oct–Apr: Tue–Sat) ▪ Adm

The largest lava tube in Portugal is a Regional Natural Monument. An astonishing 5,150 m (16,900 ft) in length, this cave is a remarkable volcanic phenomenon. Join a guided tour to walk a 450-m (1,476-ft) section bristling with stalactites, stalagmites and peculiar rock formations.

8 Museu dos Baleeiros

MAP N3 ■ Rua dos Baleeiros 13, Lajes do Pico, Pico ■ (292) 679 340 ■ Open Apr–Sep: 10am–5:30pm Tue–Sun; Oct–Mar: 9:30am–5pm Tue–Sun ■ Adm (under 14s free)

The Whalers' Museum (see p41) is a must-visit for anyone interested in the history of whaling and its social and economic impact on the islands. Before browsing the (occasionally upsetting) exhibitions, watch the documentary shot in the early 1970s – it dramatically captures a way of life that by then was already in decline.

9 Caldeira

Faial's enormous crater, 2 km (1 mile) in diameter and 400 m (1,312 ft) deep – is one of the largest in the Azores. The rim, embroidered by hydrangeas in summer, is a 7-km (4-mile) nature trail. The trailhead begins at the caldera viewpoint, which is also the start of the Ten Volcanoes Trail (see p29).

10 Capelinhos

A compulsory stop on any Faial itinerary, Capelinhos (see pp28–9) is synonymous with the events of 1957–8 when tremors and volcanic eruptions struck the area. Blanketed with lava and ash, the terrain resembles a lunar landscape. The lighthouse, Farol da Punta dos Capelinhos, survived the seismic onslaught. It stands over a futuristic-looking interpretive centre. Here the Capelinhos volcano phenomenon and volcanology is explained using film, holographic and interactive media.

Capelinhos' lunar-style landscape

A DAY EXPLORING PICO

▶ MORNING

Start your day with breakfast at **O Cinco** (see p96) in Madalena, then follow the road signs to Criação Velha. If you're visiting during the summer and want to explore the **Gruta das Torres**, the first guided tour of the cave in English commences at 9:30am. A leisurely drive along the ER-1-2 takes in the island's picturesque south coast, passing villages such as Candelária and São Caetano. To your left, the mighty Montanha do Pico is ever present, and its form changes dramatically as you head towards **Lajes do Pico** (see p93), one of the most popular destinations on the island. Take time to browse the fantastic **Museu dos Baleeiros** and then enjoy a light lunch at **Pastelaria Aromas & Sabores** (see p96).

AFTERNOON

Double back out of Lajes to Ribeira do Cabo where the EN-3 will take you up to the mountains. This is an inspiring drive, where at 700 m (2,296 ft) the landscape is all hills and pastureland. As you see a road sign to Madalena on your left, turn for a quick diversion to the enchanting **Lagoa do Capitão** (see p93). Return to the EN-3 and descend to São Roque do Pico. The **Museu da Indústria Baleeira** (see p93) is worth visiting before continuing to Santa Luzia where you take the road to the UNESCO World Heritage Site **Paisagem da Cultura da Vinha da Ilha do Pico** (see pp32–3). Stop here to visit the interpretive centre, where you can stock up on some fabulous wines before ◯ your journey back to Madalena.

See map on pp88–9 ←

The Best of the Rest: São Jorge

① Parque Florestal das Sete Fontes
MAP M1

The Seven Fountains recreational forest reserve is perfect for picnics and can be combined with a trip to Ponta dos Rosais, at the island's western tip.

Parque Florestal das Sete Fontes

② Uniqueijo
MAP N1 ▪ Beira ▪ (295) 438 274 ▪ Open 9am–5:30pm Mon–Fri (call ahead for guided tours) ▪ Adm

São Jorge's rich cheeses, regarded as the best in the Azores, are made here (see p59).

③ Casa do Parque de São Jorge
MAP P1 ▪ Estrada Regional, Norte Grande ▪ (295) 417 018 ▪ Open 9am–12:30pm & 1:30–5pm daily; closed Oct–Apr: Sat & Sun

The Caldeirinhas-Norte Grande trail (see p46) takes hikers past the Parque de São Jorge visitor's centre.

④ Grutas do Algar do Montoso
MAP N2

The little explored Montoso caves entice with the promise of a descent into the island's volcanic belly (see p95).

⑤ Topo and Ilhéu do Topo
MAP R3

São Jorge's first settlers landed at this isolated far southeastern point. There is a lighthouse on Topo, which is a protected sanctuary for birds.

⑥ Cooperativa de Artesanato Nossa Senhora da Encarnação
MAP N2 ▪ Ribeira do Nabo, nr Urzelina ▪ (295) 414 296 ▪ 9am–6pm Mon–Fri

Local women create rugs, scarves, bags and basalt jewellery (see p60) at this handicraft cooperative.

⑦ Urzelina
MAP N2

In 1808 volcanic lava engulfed the entire village except the clock tower, which still remains, marked by a plaque and a solidified lava chunk.

⑧ Calheta
MAP P2 ▪ Museum: Rua das Alcaçarias ▪ (295) 416 323 ▪ Open Apr–Sep: 10am–5:30pm Tue–Sun; Oct–Mar: 9:30am–5pm Tue–Sun ▪ Adm

The island's second-largest town is proud of its seafaring heritage. The Museu Francisco de Lacerda (see p37) is worth investigating.

⑨ Casa de Artesanato Nunes
MAP Q2 ▪ Fajã do Vimes ▪ (295) 416 717

Traditional woollen bedspreads are crafted at this workshop. Nearby is the famous Café Nunes (see p96).

⑩ Velas
MAP N1

From the harbour, stroll under the 18th-century Portão do Mar. The parish church watches over a web of cobbled streets.

Town square, Velas

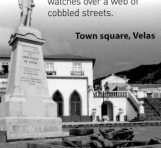

Attractions: Pico

The harbour and pretty town of Madalena

1 Madalena
MAP L2

The first port of call on the island, Madalena wins visitors over with its tidy harbour, 16th-century Igreja de Santa Maria Madalena and the acclaimed Museu do Vinho *(see p90)*.

2 Paisagem da Cultura da Vinha da Ilha do Pico

UNESCO has declared Pico's vineyards a testimony to the island's cultural tradition. The area is worthy of its World Heritage status *(see pp32–3)*.

3 Cooperativa Vitivinícola-da Ilha do Pico
MAP L2 ■ Avenida Padre Nunes da Rosa, Madalena ■ (292) 622 262 ■ Open 9am–5pm Mon–Fri (call ahead for guided tours) ■ Adm

This winery *(see p32)* creates Frei Gigante, Terras de Lava and Basalto, among other quality wines.

4 Adega A Buraca
MAP M4 ■ Estrada Regional 35, Santo António ■ (292) 642 119 ■ Open 10am–10pm Mon–Sat

Home to a museum showcasing traditional tools and farming equipments, this rustic gift shop sells local produce and includes wine tasting.

5 Lajes do Pico
MAP N3

This town is where whale watching began. The Museu dos Baleeiros *(see p91)* chronicles the timeline.

6 Museu da Indústria Baleeira
MAP N2 ■ Rua do Poço, Cais do Poço, São Roque do Pico ■ (292) 679 349 ■ Open Apr–Sep: 10am–5:30pm Tue–Sun; Oct–Mar: 9:30am–5pm Tue–Sun ■ Adm (free on Sun)

A former whaling factory is now an engaging museum, where disused machinery still fires the imagination.

7 Escola Regional de Artesanato
MAP P3 ■ Rua de Igreja 4, Santo Amaro ■ (292) 655 418 ■ Open 9am–6pm Mon–Fri (winter: to 5pm)

Visitors can buy handmade mementos at this traditional handicraft workshop and museum *(see pp60–61)*.

8 Calheta do Nesquim Trail
MAP Q3

This circular walk provides an added dimension to sightseeing in Calheta do Nesquim. The village was once a thriving whaling community.

9 Mistérios de São João
MAP M3

Leisure activities are on offer at this forest reserve, which was shaped by a volcanic eruption in 1718.

10 Lagoa do Capitão Trail
MAP N2

On a clear day Montanha do Pico *(see pp88–9)* is reflected in the "Captain's Lake", where this walk begins.

See map on pp88–9 ←

Sights: Faial

1 Fábrica da Baleia de Porto Pim

This former whaling station (see p27) shows how industrial the pursuit of whales was in the past. Also housed here is the Marine Virtual Interpretation Centre.

2 Monte da Guia
MAP J3 ■ Horta

This promontory offers fine views over Horta. A road leads to a 17th-century chapel dedicated to Senhora da Guia. The summit is closed to visitors.

3 Oceaneye
MAP J3 ■ Rua Dr Manuel Garcia Monteiro, Horta ■ (918) 395 415 ■ Timings depend on weather conditions (call ahead) ■ Adm

The glass-bottomed *Ana G* plies the shallows off Faial and Pico allowing passengers a clear view of the seabed. The trip showcases the Azores' astonishing marine biodiversity.

4 Jardim Botânico do Faial

Set in the grounds of the Quinta de São Lourenço, this garden displays endemic plants of the Azores. It includes an orchid garden too. Guided tours are available (see p27).

5 Lombega–Morro de Castelo Branco Trail
MAP H3 ■ Lombega

Ramble out of Lombega village where this walk starts. The route brings hikers up to the Castelo Branco head-land, where many seabirds reside.

6 Centro de Artesanato do Capelo
MAP G2 ■ Alto dos Cavacos, nr Capelo ■ (292) 945 027 ■ Open 9am–12:30pm & 1:30–6pm Mon & Sun, 9am–6pm Tue–Thu, 10am–5pm Fri & Sat

This school promotes local artists who can be observed creating traditional handicrafts. Terceiran embroidery is especially valued, but there are many items worth buying (see pp60–61).

7 Horta

Vibrant Horta (see pp26–7) exudes nautical bonhomie, as bobbing yachts line the marina and the lanes echo foreign tongues. Best explored on foot, Faial's only town reveals its centuries-old cultural heritage.

A windmill at Ponta da Espalamaca

8 Ponta da Espalamaca
MAP K3 ■ Espalamaca

Much photographed, the windmills dotting Espalamaca Point add colour with their red *casotas* (bonnets) topping the basalt stone bases. The outline of Pico provides a theatrical backdrop.

9 Praia do Almoxarife
MAP K3 ■ Facho

Famed for its black-sand beach – a popular summer destination – the region around Almoxarife is also noted for its picturesque valley, with grassy meadows rolling out towards the sea.

10 Parque Florestal do Capelo
MAP G2 ■ Capelo

A demanding mountain bike trail threads its way under the canopy of Capelo's recreational forest reserve. Hikers can explore at a slower pace.

Outdoor Activities

1 Vineyard Tours
Terralta Nature Tours: www.
terraltanaturetours.com
Visit wineries, find out more about
the island's grape varieties and
marvel at the UNESCO-recognized
vineyards in one of the world's most
unusual wine regions (see pp32–3).

2 Whale and Dolphin Watching
MAP N3 ■ Naturalist: www.natural
ist.pt
Pico and Faial are the best islands
for whale observation and study.
The azure ocean is also a playground
for frisky dolphins (see pp16–17).

3 Horse Riding
Pátio: www.patio.pt
Atop obedient Portuguese Lusitano
and Cruzado horses, follow ancient
paths through historic villages,
verdant forests and windblown cliffs.

4 Climbing Pico
MAP M3 ■ Tripix Azores: www.
tripixazores.com
Intrepid travellers with lots of energy
and a head for heights can scale
the summit of Portugal's highest
mountain (see pp88–9). Hiring an
official guide is recommended.

5 Nature Hikes and Walks
Aventour Azores Adventures:
www.aventour.pt
Much of São Jorge can only be
reached on foot, including a number
of fajãs (see p43) dotting the island.

Hiking in the São Jorge mountains

Regatta between Faial and Pico

6 Sailing
MAP T3 ■ Sail Azores: www.
sailazores.pt
Hoist the sails and chart a course
out of Horta to navigate the classic
triângulo – the triangular island-hop
between Faial, Pico and São Jorge.

7 Diving
MAP T3 ■ DiveAzores: www.
diveazores.net
Chilean devil rays frequent the Banco
Princesa Alice seamount (see p25), a
dive spot equidistant from Pico and
Faial. The Gruta dos Camarões, near
Horta, is famed for Narwal shrimps.

8 Kayaking
Naturfactor: www.natur
factor.com
Paddling Pico's coastline of bays,
caves and basalt rock formations
is an invigorating pastime.

9 Mountain Biking
Tripix Azores: www.tripix
azores.com
Whether negotiating mountain paths
or riding through woodlands, pro-
pelling a mountain bike off the beaten
track is one of the most exhilarating
ways of taking in island scenery.

10 Caving and Geotourism
Aventour – Azores Adventures:
www.aventour.pt
Magical and mysterious, the caves
and grottoes honeycombed deep
beneath the ground include the
immense Algar do Montoso (see p92).

See map on pp88–9 ←

Cafés and Bars

1 Café Nunes
MAP Q2 ▪ Fajã dos Vimes, São Jorge ▪ (295) 416 717

It is a long way to go for coffee, but what is poured is totally unique. They make Arabica coffee from beans grown in the village, the only place in Europe where coffee is cultivated.

Diners at Peter Café Sport

2 Peter Café Sport
MAP T3 ▪ Rua José Azevedo 9, Horta, Faial ▪ (292) 292 327

Opt for steak and grilled sardines with one of Peter's famous cocktails *(see p57)*. The fascinating Museu de Scrimshaw is upstairs *(see p40)*.

3 Café Açor
MAP N1 ▪ Rua da Matriz 41, Velas, São Jorge ▪ (295) 432 463

Centrally located, this café overlooks the square and its church. Families flock to the terrace in summer.

4 Oceanic Café
MAP J3 ▪ Rua Vasco da Gama 46A, Horta, Faial ▪ (966) 783 101 ▪ Closed Sun

Set in a historical building near the marina, this friendly café hosts live music most weekends.

5 O Cinco
MAP L2 ▪ Rua Carlos Dabney 5, Madalena, Pico ▪ (292) 623 970 ▪ Closed Sun

Vegetarians will appreciate the menu at this breezy snack bar, known for its creative and inexpensive food. The Guinness, Erdinger and Budweiser will tempt beer drinkers.

6 Pastelaria Aromas & Sabores
MAP N3 ▪ Rua Capitão Mor G.G. Madruga, Lajes do Pico, Pico ▪ (292) 672 877 ▪ Closed Sun

Sample the bakery's very own *bolo baleeiro (see p59)* or enjoy one of their sweet liqueurs. A popular breakfast and lunch venue for locals.

7 Bar Esplanade Clube Naval
MAP N2 ▪ Praceta dos Baleeiros, São Roque, Pico ▪ (292) 644 543

Handy for the São Jorge ferry, the navy club's dockside café-bar is good for a quick snack. It also makes a great coffee stop after visiting the Museu da Indústria Baleeira *(see p93)*.

8 Casa de Chá e Bar
MAP S2 ▪ Rua de São João 38A, Horta, Faial ▪ (292) 700 053 ▪ Closed Wed, Sat, Sun am

A perfect place to enjoy tea and cake in a serene garden setting, the Tea House *(see p57)* also tempts with healthy snacks plus coffee, wines and beers. The rooftop terrace is a blissful retreat.

9 Taberna de Pim
MAP T4 ▪ Rua Nova 3, Horta ▪ (912) 698 993 ▪ Closed Tue

This waterfront bistro offers a broad view of Horta's old harbour. Arrive late afternoon, order a chilled white wine and let the world catch up. If it is not busy, try the food.

10 Café Volga
MAP T3 ▪ Praça Infante Dom Henrique 16, Horta, Faial ▪ (292) 292 347 ▪ Closed Sun

There is a pleasing lack of ceremony at this informal café, making it the ideal choice for a simple snack with no trimmings. Order a *bifana* (steak sandwich) and blend in with the locals.

Restaurants

1 Fornos de Lava
MAP N1 ▪ Travessa de São Tiago 46, Santo Amaro, São Jorge ▪ (917) 394 977 ▪ Closed Wed ▪ €€

The kitchen *(see p57)* leans towards country fare but the menu also lists creative seafood dishes.

2 Amilcar
MAP P1 ▪ Fajã do Ouvidor, São Jorge ▪ (295) 417 448 ▪ Closed Tue ▪ €€

Sitting on the edge of the harbour is this cheerful little restaurant whose speciality is *ameijoas* (clams).

3 Genuíno
MAP S4 ▪ Areinha Velha 9, Angustias, Horta, Faial ▪ (292) 701 542 ▪ Closed Jan ▪ €€

Brilliantly prepared fish and seafood, a notable wine list and lovely views of Porto Pim place Genuíno *(see p56)* among the Azores' best restaurants.

4 Canto da Doca
MAP T3 ▪ Rua Nova, Horta, Faial ▪ (292) 292 444 ▪ €€

Order your meat or seafood, then cook it yourself on a hot slab of lava stone.

5 Cella Bar
MAP L2 ▪ Lugar da Barca, nr Madalena, Pico ▪ (292) 623 654 ▪ €€

This bar-restaurant's cursive, wooden skin *(see p57)* is an award-winning

The striking façade of Cella Bar

PRICE CATEGORIES
For a three-course meal for one with half a bottle of wine (or equivalent meal), taxes and extra charges.

€ under €20   €€ €20–40   €€€ over €40

modern design statement. The menu is creative, and the wine list second to none. Unbeatable views.

6 Fonte Cuisine
MAP N3 ▪ Aldeia da Fonte, Caminho de Baixo, Lajes de Pico, Pico ▪ (292) 679 500 ▪ €€

Enjoy a romantic dinner amid gardens overlooking a secluded bay. The cuisine *(see p57)* honours Portuguese culinary tradition with international flourishes.

7 Ponta da Ilha
MAP Q3 ▪ Caminho de Baixo, Manhenha, Pico ▪ (292) 666 708 ▪ Closed Wed ▪ €€

Located at the eastern tip of Pico, this restaurant serves seafood specialities such as grilled fish kebabs.

8 Vista da Baía
MAP G2 ▪ Varadouro, nr Capelo, Faial ▪ (292) 945 140 ▪ Open in summer only; closed Wed ▪ €

This is the place to visit for home-style chicken, grilled to perfection. Enjoy it with hot garlic bread and a cold beer.

9 O Esconderijo
MAP J1 ▪ Rua Janalves 3, Cedros, Faial ▪ (292) 946 505 ▪ Closed Mon & Tue ▪ €€

Come here for inventive homemade vegetarian and vegan fare served in a country cottage-style environment.

10 Ancoradouro
MAP L2 ▪ Rua Rodrigo Guerra 7, Madalena, Pico ▪ (292) 623 490 ▪ Closed Mon ▪ €€€

A picturesque waterfront location near the island's vineyards *(see pp32–3)* enhances the appeal of this noted seafood restaurant *(see p57)*.

See map on pp88–9 ⬅

📕 Flores and Corvo Islands

As the westernmost island of the Azores, Flores also marks the western extremity of Europe. Peaceful and remote, the island is dotted with lakes and waterfalls, and awash with hydrangeas in summer, their pinkish-lilac hue colouring the landscape. Flores also hosts spectacular hiking trails that wind along coastal cliffs. Neighbouring Corvo is the archipelago's smallest island, a gem moored in isolated splendour. This charming destination is shaped around an awe-inspiring, ancient caldera. These two islands are paired as UNESCO Biosphere Reserves, thanks to their diverse and pristine habitats.

Poço do Bacalhau, Flores

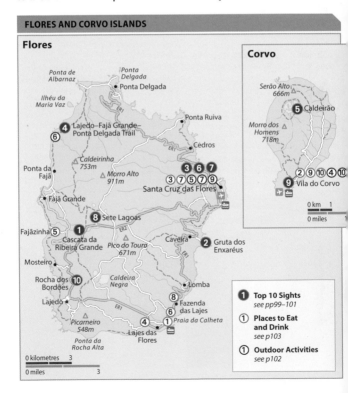

FLORES AND CORVO ISLANDS

Flores

Ponta de Albarnaz
Ilhéu da Maria Vaz
Ponta Delgada
Ponta Delgada
Ponta Ruiva
④ ⑥ Lajedo–Fajã Grande–Ponta Delgada Trail
Cedros
Caldeirinha 753m
③ ⑥ ⑦
Ponta da Fajã
△ Morro Alto 911m
③ ⑦ ⑤ ⑦ ⑨
Santa Cruz das Flores
Fajã Grande
⑧ Sete Lagoas
Fajãzinha ⑤
① Cascata da Ribeira Grande
Caveira
△ Pico do Touro 671m
② Gruta dos Enxaréus
Mosteiro
Rocha dos Bordões ⑩
Caldeira Negra
Lomba
Lajedo
⑧ Fazenda das Lajes
⑥ ① Praia da Calheta
△ Picarneiro 548m
④
Lajes das Flores
Ponta da Rocha Alta

0 kilometres 3
0 miles 3

Corvo

Serão Alto 666m
⑤ Caldeirão
Morro dos Homens 718m
② ⑨ ⑩ ④ ⑩
⑨ Vila do Corvo

0 km 1
0 miles 1

① **Top 10 Sights**
see pp99–101

① **Places to Eat and Drink**
see p103

① **Outdoor Activities**
see p102

1 Cascata da Ribeira Grande

MAP Q6 ■ Fajãzinha, Flores

Plunging hundreds of metres to roar through a natural amphitheatre of mountain greenery, the Ribeira Grande waterfall is a treat for eyes and ears. The tumbling river nourishes dozens of smaller crystalline waterfalls that plummet into lakes and ponds, including the natural lagoon, Poço do Bacalhau, or the "Codfish Pool".

Museu da Fábrica da Baleia do Boqueirão

2 Gruta dos Enxaréus

MAP R6 ■ Flores

Accessible by boat and only visible from the sea, this partly submerged cavern is 50 m (164 ft) long and 25 m (82 ft) wide. Local legend suggests that the cave served as a hideout for pirates and smugglers. Modern-day treasure hunters (and divers) can visit by joining an ocean-going excursion that also seeks out other caves and rock formations *(see p102)*.

3 Museu da Fábrica da Baleia do Boqueirão

MAP R5 ■ Rua do Boqueirão, Santa Cruz das Flores, Flores ■ (292) 542 932 ■ Open Apr–Sep: 10am–5:30pm Tue–Sun; Oct–Mar: 9:30am–5pm Tue–Sun ■ Adm

The old Boqueirão whaling station is now an excellent and extensive museum that presents the story of whaling in the Azores. Dating from the early 1940s, this was one of the largest factories of its kind and operated for over 30 years. The factory floor houses original equipment and machinery, while upstairs an interactive exhibition traces the development of the industry.

4 Lajedo–Fajã Grande–Ponta Delgada Trail

MAP Q5 ■ Flores

The Flores west-coast walk stretches 22 km (14 miles) along Europe's westernmost coastline. It is an equally exhilarating hiking challenge *(see p47)* whether starting from Lajedo or following a reverse itinerary out of Ponta Delgada. Along the way, look out for the landmark Rocha dos Bordões *(see p101)* in the south and, in the north, the Ilhéu de Monchique, the most western point of Europe. Bird-watchers should note that the largest European colonies of roseate tern nest on these islets.

Coastal landscape at Fajã Grande

Twin lakes encircled by the Caldeirão, the ancient volcanic crater

5 Caldeirão
MAP R4 ■ Corvo

A profound sense of peace can be experienced when peering into the basin of this huge crater (see p43), its allure magnified by the remote location. This is a fertile habitat for American and European migratory birds during autumn, when the island welcomes ornithologists from around the world. Follow the well-signed trail along the rim and down through pastures to the water's edge.

AUTUMN MIGRATION ON CORVO

At the very edge of the Western Palearctic, Corvo is ideally positioned as a landing stage for the autumn migration of Nearctic waders and wildfowl – North American vagrants that number a spectacular variety of rare species. Adding lustre is the high incidence of Nearctic landbirds. Among those recorded by bird-watchers are white-rumped sandpipers, rose-breasted grosbeaks and laughing gulls. There has even been a yellow-billed cuckoo (above) sighting at Vila do Corvo.

6 Museu das Flores
MAP R5 ■ Edifício do Convento de São Boaventura, Santa Cruz das Flores, Flores ■ (292) 592 159 ■ Open 9am–12:30pm & 2–5:30pm Mon–Fri ■ Adm

Its tranquil setting in the cloisters of a former 17th-century Franciscan convent encourages visitors to linger in this ethnographic museum (see p40). The island's whaling heritage is reflected in the display of scrimshaw (see p60), while the sacred art leads visitors to the adjoining church. The nearby 17th-century Casa Museu Pimentel de Mesquita is believed to be the oldest home on the island.

7 Centro de Interpretação Ambiental do Boqueirão
MAP R5 ■ Rua do Boqueirão 2A, Santa Cruz das Flores, Flores ■ (292) 542 447 ■ Open 9am–12:30pm & 1:30–5pm daily (call ahead for guided tours); closed Oct–Apr: Sat & Sun ■ Adm

Housed underground in former whale-oil storage tanks, the Boqueirão Environmental Interpretation Centre features a series of exhibition rooms, each highlighting an aspect of the island's biodiversity. There is an area dedicated to the region's resident and migratory birds, and a hall showcasing the different species of cetaceans seen off the Azores (see pp16–17). The highlight is the imaginary "Dive to the Depths" exhibit.

8 Sete Lagoas
MAP Q6 ■ Flores

Seven lakes of differing size and appearance make up Flores' stunning "lake district". Each lake is worth seeing, although Lagoa Funda merits special mention for its captivating beauty. Nearby Lagoa Rasa is smaller but equally serene, as is Lomba. The cluster of Comprida, Seca, Branca and Negra can be hiked. With a depth of 108 m (354 ft), Caldeira Negra is the deepest.

9 Centro de Interpretação Ambiental e Cultural
MAP Q4 ■ Canada do Graciosa, Vila do Corvo, Corvo ■ (292) 596 051 ■ Open 9am–12:30pm & 1:30–5pm Mon–Fri (Call ahead for guided tours) ■ Adm

Underlining the island's UNESCO Biosphere Reserve status is this cultural and environmental interpretative centre. Visitors can learn about Corvo's cultural attractions and environmental projects, including the Wild Birds Recovery Centre, home to a great virtual reality exhibit (see p102).

10 Rocha dos Bordões
MAP Q6 ■ Mosteiro, Flores

The Bordões outcrop (see p43) is a spectacular geological phenomenon and a superb example of columnar jointing. The rock appears as if coated in honey during late afternoons. Look for the *miradouro* (viewpoint) on the road between Lajedo and Mosteiro.

Rocha dos Bordões

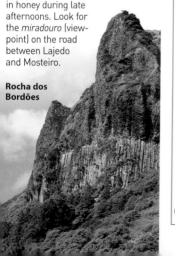

A DAY EXPLORING FLORES

Map labels: Comprida and Funda lakes, Pico da Casinda, Santa Cruz das Flores, Museu das Flores, Fajã Grande, Lucino's, Caveira, Rocha dos Bordões, Lomba, Fazenda das Lajes, Lajes das Flores

▶ MORNING

Start the day the Portuguese way with a *galão* – a large glass of hot milk with a dash of coffee – and a *tosta mista* (toasted cheese and ham sandwich) at **Lucino's** (see p103) in Santa Cruz das Flores. The drive south on the ER-1 briefly skirts the coast. Turn inland on the ER-2 for the high country, passing the Pico da Casinda lookout. Carry on until the Cruzeiro Padre Alfredo crossroads where you will see signs for the **Comprida** and **Funda lakes**. The track is narrow but suitable for vehicles. After absorbing the fabulous scenery – and taking a short walk down into the *caldeira* of Lagoa Comprida – turn back and continue on the ER-2 towards Mosteiro. You will soon have the option of turning right for **Fajã Grande** (see p99), worth a detour for the dramatic coastline. Then, double back and carry on driving south. Pull up next to the *miradouro* overlooking the amazing **Rocha dos Bordões** on your left. Afterwards, carry on to **Lajes das Flores** and pause for lunch and to explore the harbour.

AFTERNOON

A leisurely drive north out of Lajes will introduce you to the island's picturesque east coast. The meandering route snakes past scenic Fazenda das Lajes and two watermills before meeting the village of Lomba. Eventually you come to Caveira with its sweeping views of Santa Cruz, just 10 minutes away. There may still be time to visit the **Museu das Flores**.

See map on p98 ←

Outdoor Activities

1 Canyoning and Cascading
WestCanyon: www.west
canyon.pt

Landscaped with peaks, gorges, chasms and some of the highest waterfalls in the Azores, Flores is the archipelago's premier destination for adrenaline-fuelled pastimes *(see p51)*.

2 Diving
Flores Dive Center: www.
floresdivecenter.com

The scenic west coast of Flores

Famed for the abundance of dusky grouper, the Caneiro dos Meros dive site *(see p25)* off Vila do Corvo is the only voluntary marine reserve in the Azores. Those diving off Flores can explore caves such as Gruta do Galo and Gruta dos Enxaréus *(see p99)*.

3 Bird-Watching
SPEA: www.spea.pt

Resident species on the island include woodcocks, canaries and blackcaps, but during the autumn migration North American birds such as blue-winged teals and ruby-crowned kinglets are sighted. Corvo Biological Reserve attracts Cory's shearwaters *(see p53)* in summer.

Ruby-crowned kinglet

4 Centro de Reabilitação de Aves Selvagens do Corvo
MAP R4 ■ Canada do Graciosa, Vila do Corvo, Corvo ■ (292) 596 051 ■ Open 9am–12:30pm & 1:30–5pm Mon–Fri ■ Adm

The Wild Birds Recovery Centre is tasked with the rehabilitation of sick and injured birds.

5 Flores Boat Tours
MAP R5 ■ Hotel Ocidental: www.hotelocidental.com

Skirting the island's scenic coastline by boat reveals islets teeming with terns and shearwaters, and grottoes.

6 Trekking
MAP Q5 ■ WestCanyon: www.
westcanyon.pt

Trekking the west coast of Flores in summer means ambling through fields walled with bright hydrangeas. This 500-year-old footpath offers a varied and scenic hike *(see p99)*.

7 Fishing
MAP R5 ■ Zagaia Flores: www.
zagaiaflores.pt

Try your luck spinning or jigging to lure yellowmouth barracuda and other denizens of the deep.

8 Tours of Flores
Sílvio Medina: www.toursof
flores.com

Sightseeing the island by minivan taxi allows visitors to sit back as a driver steers them in the right direction.

9 Excursions to Corvo
MAP R5 ■ Passeios Turísticos: (917) 918 964/(964) 220 645

Jump aboard a rigid inflatable for a thrill-a-minute boat ride to neighbouring Corvo. The itinerary navigates selected areas of the coastline.

10 Lacticorvo
MAP R4 ■ Caminho da Horta Funda, Vila do Corvo, Corvo ■ (292) 596 005 ■ Open 9am–noon & 2–5pm Mon–Fri

Queijo do Corvo (Corvo cheese), an island delicacy, is produced at this artisan dairy. Tour the factory and sample the cheeses before buying.

Places to Eat and Drink

1 Bar O'Trancador
MAP R6 ■ Rua dos Baleeiros, Lajes das Flores, Flores ■ (931) 717 932 ■ Closed Wed ■ €

This minimalist bar has a great selection of beers and gins and offers lovely views from its terrace.

2 Irmãos Metralha
MAP R4 ■ Rua Joaquim Pedro Coelho, Vila do Corvo, Corvo ■ (292) 596 141 ■ €

A hole-in-the-wall restaurant serving great *alcatra de cabrito* (goat rump).

3 Lucino's
MAP R5 ■ Largo 25 de Abril, Santa Cruz das Flores, Flores ■ (292) 592 633 ■ €

This centrally located café-bar is a good breakfast stop for pies, cakes and sandwiches (see p57).

4 Casa do Rei
MAP R6 ■ Rua Peixoto Pimentel 33, Lajes das Flores, Flores ■ (292) 593 262 ■ Closed L; Tue ■ €€

Rustic chic describes this restaurant. The kitchen features Portuguese cuisine with meat and fish dishes.

A selection of dishes at Casa do Rei

5 Pôr do Sol
MAP Q6 ■ Fajãzinha, Flores ■ (292) 552 075 ■ Closed Mon (in summer); call for winter hours ■ €€

Try the *morcela* (black pudding) with sweet yam appetizer at this

> **PRICE CATEGORIES**
> For a three-course meal for one with half a bottle of wine (or equivalent meal), taxes and extra charges.
>
> € under €20 €€ €20–40 €€€ over €40

traditional farmhouse restaurant. Its coastal location is why the place also serves seaweed patties, a local delicacy (see p56).

6 O Forno Transmontano
MAP R6 ■ Freguesia da Fazenda das Lajes, Concelho das Lajes, Flores ■ (292) 593 137 ■ €

Enjoy a fixed menu of delicious home-cooked food. Call ahead to book a table.

7 O Moleiro
MAP R5 ■ Avenida dos Baleeiros, Santa Cruz das Flores, Flores ■ (911) 047 276 ■ €

Look past the industrial location; the menu here is value for money. Try the *cherne* (wreckfish).

8 Cana Roca
MAP R6 ■ Rua da Eirinha Vela 2, Lajes Das Flores, Flores ■ (919) 897 870 ■ €

A friendly, family-run pizzeria, Cana Roca is popular for its excellent thin-crust pizzas.

9 BBC – Caffé & Lounge
MAP R4 ■ Avenida Nova, Vila do Corvo, Corvo ■ (292) 596 030 ■ €

This friendly nightlife spot doubles up as a snack bar during the day. Impromptu live music performances are held in the evenings.

10 O Caldeirão
MAP R4 ■ Caminho dos Moinhos, Vila do Corvo, Corvo ■ (967) 548 383 ■ Closed Wed in winter ■ €

The unpretentious atmosphere at this venue is refreshing. Portions are generous and well priced.

See map on p98

Streetsmart

A scenic path along the mountains
overlooking the coast of São Miguel

Getting Around   106

Practical Information   108

Places to Stay   112

General Index   118

Acknowledgments   124

Phrase Book   126

Getting Around

Arriving by Air

Airports serve all nine islands of the Azores. **João Paulo II Airport** on São Miguel is located 3 km (2 miles) west of Ponta Delgada and is operated by **Aeroportas de Portugal**. Most international flights arrive and depart from here. **Lajes Airport** on Terceira is the Azores' second-busiest airport.

There are daily flights from most major cities in Europe and the US to Lisbon, which connect to **Horta Airport** on Faial, as well as the airports on São Miguel and Terceira.

There are daily direct flights from Lisbon's Humberto Delgado International Airport to Ponta Delgada with **Azores Airlines**, which also flies daily out of Porto, with Tuesday and Sunday flights to Lajes.

TAP Air Portugal flies from Lisbon and Porto to Ponta Delgada and Lajes on a daily basis. Low-cost carrier **Ryanair** also flies from Lisbon and Porto to Ponta Delgada and Lajes. It operates direct flights from London Stansted and (weekly) Manchester in the UK to Ponta Delgada. Azores Airlines has direct flights from Boston and Toronto to Ponta Delgada and Terceira.

Arriving by Sea

The **Portas do Mar** maritime terminal at Ponta Delgada is the first port of call for visitors arriving at São Miguel by cruise ship and inter-island ferries. The facility also extends to a recreational marina, which provides berths for over 600 boats.

On Horta the **Porto da Horta** cruise ship terminal and commercial quay is located 1 km (half a mile) northeast of the town centre. The marina, the most popular in the Azores for transatlantic yachts, is sited along the esplanade.

Terceira's cruise port facility is at **Praia da Vitória** on the western coast of the island, 20 km (12 miles) from Angra do Heroísmo.

Besides the marinas at Ponta Delgada, Horta and Praia da Vitória, there are also smaller facilities at Angra do Heroísmo, Vila do Porto, Madalena, Velas and Lajes do Pico. Ports and marinas fall under the umbrella of the **Portos dos Açores**.

Island-hopping by Air

All nine islands are linked by Azores Airlines, which operates scheduled flights around the archipelago. Flights should be booked well in advance during summer. Adverse weather can disrupt timetables, so for extensive island-hopping, insure against delays. Most flights operating between the islands take about 30 to 40 minutes, except São Miguel to Flores, which takes 1 hour 20 minutes. With an international Azores Airlines air ticket visitors can book inter-island routes online and receive a discount on fares.

Island-hopping by Sea

A network of ferries operated by **Atlanticoline** links all the islands, allowing visitors to explore the archipelago by sea.

Throughout the year there are several daily sailings between Horta and Pico by passenger and car ferries. Between April and September, there is a daily Horta–Velas service via Pico and some via São Roque. Pico, Faial and São Jorge are closely clustered – the so-called "triangle" – making it possible to plan your own island-hopping itineraries between the three islands. There are also seasonal services between Faial, Pico and São Jorge to Angra do Heroísmo. Less frequent are sailings between São Miguel and Santa Maria and the Central Group, including Graciosa, and Flores, in the Western Group. However, a regular operation exists between Flores and Corvo.

Atlanticoline has a Sea Pass (four one-way trips) and also offers concessions, including discounts for families, students and passengers with limited mobility.

Bus

Travelling the islands by public transport requires patience and flexibility. Many of the routes are designed for locals and scheduled around working hours, which might be inconvenient for tourists. There are no public transport services operating between João Paulo II Airport and Ponta Delgada town centre. Travellers have to use taxis or hire vehicles. However, São Miguel offers the most extensive bus services, allowing visitors to travel out early from Ponta Delgada and spend a day sightseeing in places such as Sete Cidades, Ribeira Grande, Nordeste and Furnas. Timetables are available from the tourist office or online at **S. Miguel Transportes**. Private bus company **Transportes de Santa Maria** provides services in Santa Maria. **Farias** operates on Faial. **Empresa de Viação Terceirense (EVT)** serves Terceira while **Cristiano Limitada** serves

Pico. The network on Flores is run by **União de Transportes dos Carvalhos (UTC)**; time-tables are displayed online. For services on Graciosa and São Jorge, consult the tourist office. There are no bus services operating on Corvo.

Taxi

Taxis in the Azores are numerous and relatively inexpensive. Trips are usually metered, although there are fixed charges for certain routes. At tourist offices, ask for lists of local taxi opera-tors. An island tour by taxi is a popular sightseeing option. Taxis are also a useful way of accessing walks. Many private taxi operators such as

Azorean Tours offer full- or half-day programmes following a fixed itinerary.

Driving

The easiest and most reliable way to get around the islands is by car. There are many car-hire companies in the Azores including **Ilha Verde** and **Autatlantis**, which have offices at airports and various towns across the archipelago. To hire a car you will need to have a valid driving licence and a passport or other form of official identification. Rates tend to be cheaper in the low season. You can also rent a scooter, which is a far cheaper method of transporta-tion and requires all the necessary documentation.

DIRECTORY

ARRIVING BY AIR

Aeroportas de Portugal
w ana.pt

Azores Airlines
((296) 209 720
w azoresairlines.pt

Horta Airport, Faial
((292) 943 511
w aeroportohorta.pt

João Paulo II Airport, São Miguel
((296) 205 400
w aeroportoponta delgada.pt

Lajes Airport, Terceira
((295) 545 494
w aerogarelajes.azores. gov.pt

Ryanair
((0871) 246 0000 (UK)
w ryanair.com

TAP Air Portugal
((211) 234 400,
(0345) 350 0100
w flytap.com

ARRIVING BY SEA

Portos dos Açores
w portosdosacores.pt

Portas do Mar
((296) 281 500
w portosdosacores.pt

Porto da Horta
((292) 391 693
w portosdosacores.pt

Praia da Vitória
((295) 105 134

ISLAND-HOPPING BY SEA

Atlanticoline
((292) 242 000
w atlanticoline.pt

BUS

Cristiano Limitada
w cristianolimitada.pt

Empresa de Viação Terceirense (EVT)
w evt.pt

Farias
w farias.pt

S. Miguel Transportes
w smigueltransportes. com

Transportes de Santa Maria
w transportesdesanta maria.com

Uniao de Transportes dos Carvalhos (UTC)
w utc.pt

TAXI

Azorean Tours
w azoreantours.com

DRIVING

Autatlantis
((296) 205 340
w autatlantis.com

Ilha Verde
((296) 304 891
w ilhaverde.com

Practical Information

Passports and Visas

For entry requirements, including visas, consult your nearest Portuguese embassy or check the Portuguese **Ministry of Foreign Affairs**. European Union (EU) nationals and citizens of the UK, US, Canada, Australia and New Zealand do not need visas for stays of up to three months; non-EU nationals must have passports valid for at least three months beyond their planned departure date.

Embassies and consulates located in Ponta Delgada and Lisbon, including those of the **UK**, **US**, **Canada** and **Australia**, provide services for nationals visiting the Azores.

Government Advice

Now more than ever, it is important to consult both your and the Portuguese government's advice before travelling. The **UK Foreign, Commonwealth & Development Office (FCDO)**, the **US Department of State**, the **Australian Department of Foreign Affairs and Trade** and the **Câmara Municipal de Lisboa** offer the latest information on security, health and local regulations.

Customs Information

It is illegal to export scrimshaw and other items made from whale teeth and bone. For EU citizens, there are limits on goods taken into or out of the country for personal use. You can find information on the laws relating to goods and currency taken in or out of Portugal on the **Visa HQ** website.

Insurance

Taking out a comprehensive insurance policy covering theft, loss of belongings, medical care, trip-cancellations and delays is recommended. Adventure tourists can purchase additional cover for high-risk activities such as watersports, horse riding and canyoning.

UK and EU citizens are eligible for free emergency medical care in Portugal provided they have a valid **EHIC** (European Health Insurance Card) or **GHIC** (UK Global Health Insurance Card).

Health

Portugal has a world-class healthcare system. Emergency medical care in Portugal is free for all UK and EU citizens. If you have an EHIC or GHIC, be sure to present this in a medical emergency. You may have to pay after treatment and reclaim the money later. For visitors from outside the EU and Australia, payment of expenses is the patient's responsibility, so it is important to arrange comprehensive medical insurance before travelling.

Healthcare facilities are basic outside the main towns. Walk-in health centres, known as *centros de saúde*, provide check-ups and non-emergency treatment. The **Centro de Saúde de Santa Cruz das Flores** has a hyperbaric chamber. *Farmácias* (pharmacies) are widespread and identified by their green cross signage. Tap water is safe to drink; however, water sourced from fountains should be avoided, particularly those noted as *água não potável* (not suitable for drinking). For information regarding COVID-19 vaccination requirements, consult government advice. No other vaccinations are required to enter Portugal, but routine vaccines should be kept up-to-date.

Personal Security

The Azores are considered a safe destination for visitors, but it is still wise to take precautions against theft. Keep your valuables in a safe place when in your accommodation and on you at all other times.

Theft should be reported to the authorities as soon as possible. You will need an official police report signed to present to your insurers in order to make a claim. There is a 24-hour **Tourist Police** division in Ponta Delgada. Theft or loss of documents, such as your passport, should also be reported to your consulate. The police, ambulance and fire brigade can be reached on the nationwide emergency number 112. The operators speak English and calls are free.

The Portuguese are generally accepting of all people, regardless of their race, gender or sexuality. Homosexuality was legalized in 1982 and in 2010, Portugal became the eighth country in the world to recognize same-sex marriage. Portugal prides itself on being a tolerant country; homophobic attitudes are very much the exception, not the norm. Having said this, some rural areas remain conservatively Catholic, and public displays of affection may be met with hostility. If you do feel unsafe, the **Safe Space Alliance** pinpoints your nearest point of refuge.

Women may receive unwanted attention, especially around tourist areas. If you feel threatened, head straight for the nearest police station.

Travellers with Specific Requirements

The Azores are slowly addressing the requirements of travellers with limited mobility. Azores Airlines *(see p107)* offers ground and in-flight assistance to passengers with specific requirements. Similarly, TAP Air Portugal *(see p107)* offers a departure-to-arrival service. **Accessible Portugal** can arrange hotel and airport transfers using vehicles adapted for wheelchairs. **Disabled Holidays** lists hotels suitable for guests with limited mobility and can arrange travel insurance which caters for disabilities and pre-existing medical conditions. **Cresaçor** *(see p15)* is a pioneer of inclusive tourism in the archipelago and is listed on the **European Network for Accessible Tourism**. Some restaurants are adapting their facilities to meet the demands of wheelchair-bound diners, as are selected museums, some of which also provide information in Braille. It is always wise to call ahead and check.

DIRECTORY

PASSPORTS AND VISAS

Australian Embassy
Avenida da Liberdade 200, 2nd Floor, Lisbon, Portugal
📞 (213) 101 500

British Consulate General
Rua de São Bernardo 33, Lisbon, Portugal
📞 (213) 924 000

Canadian Embassy
Avenida da Liberdade 198–200, 3rd Floor, Lisbon, Portugal
📞 (213) 164 600

Ministry of Foreign Affairs
🌐 vistos.mne.gov.pt

United States Consulate General
MAP U1 ■ Avenida Príncipe do Mónaco 6, Ponta Delgada, São Miguel
📞 (296) 308 330

GOVERNMENT ADVICE

Australian Department of Foreign Affairs and Trade
🌐 dfat.gov.au
🌐 smartraveller.gov.au

Câmara Municipal de Lisboa
🌐 visitar.lisboa.pt

UK Foreign, Commonwealth & Development Office (FCDO)
🌐 gov.uk/foreign-travel-advice

US Department of State
🌐 travel.state.gov

CUSTOMS INFORMATION

Visa HQ
🌐 visahq.com/portugal

INSURANCE

EHIC
🌐 ec.europa.eu

GHIC
🌐 ghic.org.uk

HEALTH

Centro de Saúde de Santa Cruz das Flores
MAP R5 ■ Largo 25 de Abril, Santa Cruz das Flores, Flores
📞 (292) 590 270

PERSONAL SECURITY

Tourist Police
MAP V2 ■ Rua da Alfândega, Ponta Delgada, São Miguel
📞 (296) 205 500

Safe Space Alliance
🌐 safespacealliance.com

TRAVELLERS WITH SPECIFIC REQUIREMENTS

Accessible Portugal
🌐 accessibleportugal.com

Cresaçor
🌐 azoresforall.com

Disabled Holidays
🌐 disabledholidays.com

European Network for Accessible Tourism
🌐 accessibletourism.org

Time Zone

The islands are 1 hour behind Greenwich Mean Time (GMT) and 4 hours ahead of US Eastern Standard Time (EST). The clock moves forward 1 hour during daylight saving time, from the last Sunday in March to the last Sunday in October.

Money

Portugal's unit of currency is the euro. Banknotes of denominations greater than €50 are not widely circulated or readily accepted as payment. Some establishments prefer to work with smaller denominations. Currency exchange is available at **Nova Câmbios** in Ponta Delgada airport and most banks: look for the desks marked *câmbios*. Banking hours are 8:30am to 3pm Monday to Friday. The most convenient way of getting funds is via an ATM, known as *multibanco* or MB. These are located in and outside most banks, public transport hubs and shopping centres. Traveller's cheques are not widely accepted.

Without a credit card, you will not be able to rent a car or check in to a hotel. MasterCard and visa are accepted everywhere; American Express and Diners Club cards less so.

Electrical Appliances

The islands use plugs with two round pins and a voltage of 220V. Most hotels offer built-in adaptors for electric razors.

Mobile Phones and Wi-Fi

The country code for Portugal is 00351. The islands also have individual codes: 296 for São Miguel and Santa Maria; 295 for Terceira, Graciosa and São Jorge; 292 for Pico, Faial, Flores and Corvo. Most telephone booths accept a *cartão telefónico* (telephone chargecard), available at post offices, kiosks and newsagents.

Many of the islands' hotels offer Wi-Fi. Internet access is also available at Ponta Delgada, Lajes and Horta airports and in lots of bars, cafés, restaurants and larger shopping malls. To use your mobile phone in the Azores, it will need to be equipped for GSM network frequencies 900 and 1800 MHz. Find out more on **Frequency Check**. To avoid roaming fees, purchase a local SIM card. Check with your home carrier for international package deals and if you need to unlock your device to use a different SIM card/service.

Mail

The Portuguese postal service is known as the **CTT Correios de Portugal**. *Correios* (post offices) are usually open from 9am to 6pm on weekdays. First-class mail, known as *correio azul*, is posted in blue postboxes, everything else in red postboxes.

Weather

An all-year destination, the Azores enjoy a mild temperate climate, with the average temperature varying between 11° C and 26° C (51° F and 78° F). June, July and August are the warmest months. April, May, September and October have pleasant weather. November to March can see wet, windy days with sporadic sunshine. However, the Azores are prone to rainfall at any time of the year.

The high season runs from mid-June to mid-September when festivals and events are held all over the island; more cafés, restaurants and bars are open too.

Opening Hours

Shops are generally open from 9am to 1pm and 2 to 6pm from Monday to Friday and 9am to 1:30pm on Saturday. In the towns, business hours at larger stores often carry through the lunch hour. Shopping malls such as Parque Atlântico remain open from 9am to 11pm daily. In rural areas, shops are likely to be closed on weekends.

The COVID-19 pandemic proved that situations can change suddenly. Always check before visiting attractions and hospitality venues for up-to-date hours and booking requirements.

Visitor Information

The **Visit Azores** website provides a list of tourist offices, approved accommodation, sightseeing and practical information.

Azores Trails lists walking routes, while **Parques Naturais** describes the islands' natural parks and the the **Sentir e Interpretar o Ambiente dos Açores** provides details on the flora and fauna – and unusual landscapes – of the nine islands. The **Tourist Helpline** provides a good overview of the region. **Spot Azores** offers information about the weather. The **Percursos do Artesanato dos Açores** app provides lists of handicraft shops and workshops. The blogs posted on **Epicure and Culture** showcase Azorean handicraft culture and artisanal cuisine.

Trips and Tours

Well-established UK tour operators offering trips to the Azores include **Archipelago Choice** and **Sunvil**. **Biosphere Expeditions** and **Nature Trek** lean towards a more scientific and conservational experience while **Portugal Walks** organizes self-guided walks. US-based **Tour Azores** provides independent and escorted tours. **Melo Agência de Viagens** in Ponta Delgada offers walking holidays. **Responsible Travel** specializes in nature and environmental tourism.

Language

Portuguese is the official language in the Azores. English is widely spoken in most towns, cities and tourist resorts, but it is less prevalent in rural areas.

Accommodation

There are several five-star hotels in São Miguel and one in Terceira. Many historic hotels – converted forts, manor houses and convent buildings – offer upscale accommodation. The majority fall within the mid-range, four-star category. Numerous B&Bs and traditionally styled guesthouses are listed on the **Casas Açorianas** website. Budget travellers can opt for one- and two-star hotels known as a *pensão* or *residencial*. Another idea is to check into a hostel or book on **Airbnb.** There are five youth hostels operated by **Azores Pousadas de Juventude**. All islands have official campsites; the Visit Azores website lists most.

DIRECTORY

MONEY

Nova Câmbios
MAP B6 ■ João Paulo II Airport, Ponta Delgada, São Miguel
■ Open 7am–9pm Mon–Fri, 7am–2pm & 3–5pm Sat & Sun
[(296) 306 770

MOBILE PHONES AND WI-FI

Frequency Check
w frequencycheck.com

MAIL

CTT Correios de Portugal
w ctt.pt

VISITOR INFORMATION

Azores Trails
w trails.visitazores.com

Epicure and Culture
w epicureandculture.com

Parques Naturais
w parquesnaturais. azores.gov.pt

Percursos do Artesanato dos Açores
w artesanato.azores. gov.pt

Sentir e Interpretar o Ambiente dos Açores
w siaram.azores.gov.pt

Spot Azores
w spotazores.com

Tourist Helpline
[(296) 284 569

Visit Azores
w visitazores.com

TRIPS AND TOURS

Archipelago Choice
w archipelagochoice.com

Biosphere Expeditions
w biosphere-expeditions.org

Melo Agência de Viagens
w melotravel.com

Nature Trek
w naturetrek.co.uk

Portugal Walks
w portugalwalks.com

Responsible Travel
w responsibletravel.com

Sunvil
w sunvil.co.uk

Tour Azores
w tourazores.com

ACCOMMODATION

Airbnb
w airbnb.com

Azores Pousadas de Juventude
w pousadasjuva cores.com

Casas Açorianas
w casasacorianas.com

Places to Stay

PRICE CATEGORIES

For a standard double room in high season, including taxes and extra charges.

€ under €70   €€ €70–150   €€€ over €150

Historic Hotels

Casa do Campo de São Francisco

MAP U2 ■ Campo de São Francisco 15–17, Ponta Delgada, São Miguel ■ (296) 287 144 ■ www.casacamposaofrancisco.com ■ €€

This impressive 18th-century mansion features antique furnishings. The building has three rooms and two suites decorated to reflect the Baroque period. Breakfast is a feast of Azorean produce laid out on tiled tabletops.

Convento de São Francisco

MAP D6 ■ Jardim António Silva Cabral, Vila Franca do Campo, São Miguel ■ (962) 651 593 ■ www.conventosaofrancisco.net ■ €€€

A perfect place for those seeking peace and solitude, this former 16th-century convent has been renovated as an elegant retreat. Each room is decorated with contemporary and religious art, wood and rich fabrics.

Hotel do Colégio

MAP U2 ■ Rua Carvalho Araújo 39, Ponta Delgada, São Miguel ■ (296) 306 600 ■ www.hotelcolegio.pt ■ €€

The beautiful vaulted ceilings that grace the lounge and bar add historic character to this attractive hotel. The building dates from the 19th century and was previously a music conservatory.

Pousada Forte Angra do Heroísmo

MAP M6 ■ Rua do Castelinho, Angra do Heroísmo, Terceira ■ (295) 403 560 ■ www.pousadas.pt ■ €€

Located behind the walls of the former Castelo de São Sebastião on a dramatic coastline are 28 modern rooms and one suite of exceptional character. The most atmospheric are those housed in the refurbished governor's house.

Quinta de Nossa Senhora das Mercês

MAP M6 ■ Caminho de Baixo, São Mateus, Angra do Heroísmo, Terceira ■ (295) 642 588 ■ www.quintadasmerces.com ■ €€

This grand country manor was built in the 17th century. In keeping with its historical patrimony, the hotel features classically styled rooms. The highlight is the infinity pool with its Atlantic panorama.

Quinta do Espírito Santo

MAP M6 ■ Rua Dr Teotónio Machado Pires 36, Angra do Heroísmo, Terceira ■ (295) 332 373 ■ www.quintadoespiritosanto.com ■ €€

Owner Francisco Maduro-Dias is the former director for the office of restoration of Angra do Heroísmo's World Heritage Site. Together with his wife, he welcomes guests to their gorgeous home, an 18th-century landmark.

Solar de Lalém

MAP D5 ■ Estrada de São Pedro, Maia, São Miguel ■ (296) 442 004 ■ www.solardelalem.com ■ €€

A beautifully preserved 1687-built chapel dedicated to São Sebastião is the oldest part of this property. Once the residence of 17th-century aristocrats, the manor house features individually decorated rooms with antique furnishings.

Pousada Forte da Horta

MAP T3 ■ Rua Vasco da Gama, Horta, Faial ■ (210) 407 670 ■ www.pousadas.pt ■ €€€

Once impregnable, the 16th-century Forte de Santa Cruz is today a charming hotel overlooking Horta's harbour and the colourful marina. The Sal & Pico Restaurant serves regional cuisine with wines from Portugal.

Terra Nostra Garden Hotel

MAP E5 ■ Rua Padre José Jacinto Botelho 5, Furnas, São Miguel ■ (296) 549 090 ■ www.bensaudehotels.com ■ €€€

Dating back to the 1930s, this is one of the most emblematic hotels in the Azores. The original building still retains Art Deco flourishes. Residents enjoy free access to the famous 18th-century park.

Eco and Nature Hotels

7 Cidades Lake Lodge
MAP A5 ▪ Rua das Lavadeiras 2, Sete Cidades, São Miguel ▪ (918) 304 014 ▪ www.7cidadeslake lodge.com ▪ €€

Stay in lakefront bungalows set on the tranquil shores of Lagoa Azul. The wood-wrapped accommodation blends perfectly with the environment and provides all modern conveniences.

Aldeia da Cuada
MAP R6 ▪ Aldeia da Cuada, Lajes do Flores, Flores ▪ (292) 552 127 ▪ www.aldeiadacuada. com ▪ €€

This once-abandoned village of 14 stone cottages is now one of the Azores' most celebrated rural resorts. The buildings have been refurbished as fully equipped one-, two-and six-bedroom units.

Aldeia da Fonte
MAP N3 ▪ Caminho de Baixo, Silveira, Lajes do Pico, Pico ▪ (292) 679 500 ▪ www.aldeiadafonte. com ▪ €€

These volcanic stone cottages on a cliffside house studios, rooms and suites. Nights see the arrival of Azores noctule bats, the archipelago's only endemic mammal.

Jardim do Triângulo
MAP N1 ▪ Eco Triângulo, Terreiros 91, Velas, São Jorge ▪ (295) 414 055 ▪ www.ecotriangulo. com ▪ €€

A complimentary bottle of wine is offered to guests along with the keys to their basalt stone cottages, set

over a landscaped garden in the grounds of an 18th-century country house.

Quinta da Meia Eira
MAP H3 ▪ Rua dos Inocentes 1, Castelo Branco, Horta, Faial ▪ (965) 435 925 ▪ www. meiaeira.com ▪ €€

Bright and colourful, this family-run farmhouse features cottages and rooms that are traditionally furnished and surrounded by lovely gardens. The solarium is a winter bonus.

Quinta das Buganvílias
MAP H3 ▪ Quinta das Buganvílias 28A, Castelo Branco, Faial ▪ (292) 943 255 ▪ www.quintadas buganvilias.com ▪ €€

Accommodation here is on a well-maintained organic farm. Rooms are available in the main building and the stone annexe. The grounds feature a variety of flowers, along with guava and banana trees.

Quinta da Terça
MAP C6 ▪ Rua Padre Domingos 221, Livramento, São Miguel ▪ (296) 642 134 ▪ www. quintadaterca.com ▪ €€

An equestrian theme runs through this farmhouse, which is part of a working stable. It is geared towards riders seeking a base from which to explore the island. Complimentary breakfast included.

Quinta do Martelo
MAP M6 ▪ Canada do Martelo 24, São Mateus, Terceira ▪ (962) 812 796 ▪ www.quintadomartelo. net ▪ €€

Guests can experience a unique countryside stay at this charming

homestead. Four types of accommodation options are available, including the cosy "settler's houses".

Pestana Bahia Praia – Nature & Beach Resort
MAP D6 ▪ Praia de Água d'Alto, Vila Franca do Campo, São Miguel ▪ (296) 539 130 ▪ www. pestana.com ▪ €€€

During summer, guests are regaled by the nasal cries of Cory's shear-waters nesting on nearby cliffs, a sea-life sound-track that adds appeal to this secluded resort. Splendid oceanside views embrace a sandy bay.

Santa Bárbara Eco-Beach Resort
MAP C5 ▪ Estrada Regional 1, Morro de Baixo-Ribeira Seca, São Miguel ▪ (296) 470 360 ▪ www.santa barbaraazores.com ▪ €€€€

Located along an idyllic coastline, this villa com-plex features minimalist architectural design. A restaurant, bar and beach club add to the experience.

Contemporary Hotels

INATEL Graciosa Resort & Business Hotel
MAP K5 ▪ Porto da Barra, Santa Cruz da Graciosa, Graciosa ▪ (295) 730 500 ▪ www.hoteis.inatel.pt ▪ €€

Flanked by vineyards and with views over the bay of Cais da Barra, accom-modation here includes rooms, suites and villas. Leisure facilities extend to a pool and sauna, while the Remember Azores (see p85) restaurant adds a dash of sophistication.

Hotel Colombo
MAP E2 ■ Lugar da Cruz Teixeira, Vila do Porto, Santa Maria ■ (296) 820 200 ■ www.colombo-hotel.com ■ €€

Hugely popular in the summer months, this hotel has plenty of amenities to keep guests occupied, including a pool, Jacuzzi and Turkish bath. There is also a play park for kids.

INATEL Flores Hotel
MAP R5 ■ Zona do Boqueirão, Santa Cruz das Flores, Flores ■ (292) 590 420 ■ www.hoteis.inatel.pt ■ €€

All 26 rooms at this hotel near the whaling museum have superb views of distant Corvo. The interior is decorated with black-and-white images of whales, sharks and other marine life. A great bar, restaurant and outside pool complete the picture.

Hotel do Canal
MAP T3 ■ Largo Dr Manuel de Arriaga, Horta, Faial ■ (292) 202 120 ■ www.bensaudehotels.com ■ €€

Rooms facing the harbour offer inspiring views of the marina and nearby Pico – a breathtaking panorama at any time of the day. Located in the town centre, the hotel's amenities include a fitness centre, a sauna and the Clipper Restaurant.

Hotel Terceira Mar
MAP M6 ■ Portões de São Pedro, Angra do Heroísmo, Terceira ■ (295) 402 280 ■ www.bensaude hotels.com ■ €€

Not far from the UNESCO-listed historic centre, this handsome property overlooks a bay. A health club, an outdoor seawater pool and the Monte Brasil Restaurant encourage rest and relaxation. The hotel is noted for its environmental management.

Hotel Vila Nova
MAP U2 ■ Rua João Francisco Cabral 1/3, Ponta Delgada, São Miguel ■ (296) 301 600 ■ www.mystoryhotels.com ■ €€

Comfortable and functional, this modern hotel is ideal for families and business travellers seeking a base near the historic centre. A breakfast and dinner buffet is offered. Guests can take advantage of an outdoor pool.

Azoris Royal Garden
MAP U2 ■ Rua de Lisboa, Ponta Delgada, São Miguel ■ (296) 307 300 ■ www.azorishotels.com.com ■ €€€

Accommodation at this upscale hotel includes spacious, well-appointed family rooms. It is also possible to place an extra cot or assemble a daybed in the senior suite. Business travellers will appreciate the meetings and events facilities.

Azor
MAP V2 ■ Avenida Dr João Bosco Mota Amaral, São Miguel ■ (296) 249 900 ■ www.azorhotel.com ■ €€€€

Stay at this hotel for its cutting-edge interior design and wonderful views from the rooms. The Azor raises the bar with first-rate amenities, such as the daringly stylish rooftop pool. Downstairs, the Lobby Market combines a fabulous restaurant with an innovative Wine & Cheese Corner.

Caloura Hotel Resort
MAP C6 ■ Rua do Jublieu 27, Água de Pau, São Miguel ■ (296) 960 900 ■ www.calourahotel.com ■ €€€

This resort is set over a secluded bay with direct access both to the sea and a cluster of natural pools surrounded by volcanic rock. There is also a freshwater pool. Rooms and suites have splendid ocean views, and the in-house Barrocas do Mar Restaurant offers a wide choice of meat and seasonal fish dishes.

Pedras do Mar Resort & Spa
MAP B5 ■ Rua da Terça 3, Fenais da Luz, São Miguel ■ (296) 249 300 ■ www.pedrasdomar.com ■ €€€

An airport shuttle service whisks guests off to this peaceful resort, located on the water's edge. Family-orientated, the place has a relaxed vibe that is accentuated by its sports amenities and a modest spa facility. The out-of-the-way location, however, means you will need a vehicle to explore further.

WHITE
MAP C6 ■ Rua Rocha Quebrada 10, Lagoa, São Miguel ■ (296) 249 153 ■ www.whiteazores.com ■ €€€

Set right on the clifftop, this hotel is housed in an 18th-century building. The on-site restaurant serves dishes prepared with ingredients from their own organic farm. There's also a serene spa.

B&Bs

Guest House Comodoro
MAP R4 ■ Caminho do Areeiro, Vila do Corvo, Corvo ■ (292) 596 128 ■ www.comodoro azores.com ■ €

Renowned for its hospitality, this is still the only decent accommodation option on tiny Corvo. The guesthouse has 13 rooms, five with wooden deck terraces. Guests can request a free transfer from the airport. Book ahead for summer and autumn stays.

Casa das Faias
MAP K5 ■ Rua Infante D. Henrique 10, Praia, Graciosa ■ (295) 732 766 ■ €€

Wrapped in patterned basalt stonework, the features of this rambling inn resemble those of a rustic hotel, despite being located just a short distance out of town. The lounge on the top floor affords a lovely panoramic view of the bay. Breakfast is sometimes an ad-hoc affair, where you make your own from a freshly stocked fridge.

Casa do António
MAP N1 ■ Rua Infante D. Henrique 21, Velas, São Jorge ■ (295) 432 006 ■ Closed Dec & Jan ■ www.casadoantonio. com ■ €€

Every floor of this B&B affords a wonderful view, but the rooms facing Pico island paint a picture of serenity. Its blue-and-white façade is easily discernible from the harbour. The buffet-style breakfast served here is wholesome and plentiful.

Pensão Francisca
MAP E2 ■ Brejo de Baixo, Almagreira, Santa Maria ■ (296) 884 033 ■ www. azorean-spirit.com ■ €€

Spotless rooms and a separate cottage are on offer here, all within walking distance of the Praia Formosa beach (see pp68–9). The hosts can arrange outdoor activities, including yoga.

Quinta do Canavial
MAP M1 ■ Quinta do Canavial, Velas, São Jorge ■ (295) 412 981 ■ www. aquintadocanavial.com ■ €€

The owners of this traditional guesthouse are keen hikers and have compiled a local walking guide for their guests. The breakfast patio peers over a secluded bay and there is a seasonal pool sunk into the terrace.

Residencia Argonauta
MAP Q6 ■ Rua Senador André de Freitas 5, Fajã Grande, Flores ■ (297) 552 219 ■ Closed 1 Nov–19 Dec ■ www.argo nauta-flores.com ■ €€

Decorated with prints, photographs and various collectibles, rooms in this quirky house are adorned with volcanic rock and wood. Dating from 1929, the building still features the first bathroom built in the village.

Solar da Glória ao Carmo
MAP C6 ■ Rua da Glória ao Carmo 5, Livramento, Ponta Delgada, São Miguel ■ (296) 629 847 ■ www.gloriaaocarmo. com ■ €€

One double room, two spacious suites and a pair of custom-built apartments provide accommodation at this 18th-century manor. The breakfast changes daily and can be had at any hour of the day.

Vila Bélgica
MAP J3 ■ Caminho Velho de Caldeira 13, Horta, Faial ■ (292) 392 614 ■ www.azoresvilabelgica. com ■ €€

On a clear day, views of neighbouring Pico island from this cosy B&B are memorable. So, too, is the warm welcome from the Belgian owners. There are scenic walks on offer right from the doorstep.

Vivenda da Saudade
MAP M6 ■ Estrada Regional 14, São Mateus da Calheta, Angra do Heroísmo, Terceira ■ (295) 643 105 ■ Open Jun–Sep ■ www.vivenda saudade.com ■ €€

A rural location with sea views is reason enough to stay at this immaculately maintained B&B. The fact that it is a 10-minute drive from Angra do Heroísmo is a plus, but the amiable hosts, Al and Vilma, are the deal clincher.

Whale'come Residencial
MAP N3 ■ Rua dos Baleeiros, Lajes do Pico, Pico ■ (292) 672 010 ■ www.espacotalassa. com ■ €€

Anchored to the Espaço Talassa whale-watching operation (see p17), this maritime-themed residencial features bright breezy rooms with modern amenities. It is incredibly popular, so you need to book early, even in winter.

For a key to hotel price categories see p112

Boutique Hotels

The Azores Wine Company
MAP L2 ▪ Rua do Poço Velho, Cais do Mourato, Pico ▪ (292) 098 070 ▪ www.azoreswine company.com ▪ €€€
Stylish low-slung accommodation – five studios and a two-bed-room apartment – set amid the corrals of Pico's vineyards. Try revived varieties from the on-site winery *(see p33)*.

Hotel Charming Blue
MAP E2 ▪ Rua Teófilo de Braga 31, Vila do Porto, Santa Maria ▪ (296) 882 083 ▪ www.charming blue.com ▪ €€
The classical veneer belies the modernity of this lovely townhouse. Rooms are contemporary and elegantly designed, and the restaurant sets new culinary standards. Other amenities include a modest spa.

Hotel Praia Marina
MAP P5 ▪ Avenida Alvaro Martins Homen, Praia da Vitória, Terceira ▪ (295) 540 055 ▪ www.hotel praiamarina.com ▪ €€
Bright, modern studio apartments offer splendid balcony views over the beach and the nearby marina. Functional and reliable, the hotel is just a short walk from the town centre.

Hotel Talisman
MAP U2 ▪ Rua Marquês da Praia e Monforte 40, Ponta Delgada, São Miguel ▪ (296) 308 505 ▪ www.hoteltalisman. com ▪ €€
Centrally located, the building dates back to the 17th century and retains its period charm, exemplified by the romantic Palm Terrace Restaurant. The guest experience here is heightened by a sun-trapping rooftop pool.

Pico do Refúgio
MAP C5 ▪ Roda do Pico 5, Rabo de Peixe, Ribeira Grande, São Miguel ▪ (296) 491 062 ▪ www. picodorefugio.com ▪ €€
A 17th-century country manor house has been carefully refurbished into superbly appointed apartments and lofts. Guests can walk the farmland (an ecological reserve) and there is even an on-site diving school. Ideal for couples and families.

Baía da Barca
MAP L2 ▪ Lugar da Barca, Madalena, Pico ▪ (292) 628 750 ▪ www.baiada barca.com ▪ €€€
Seemingly chiselled out of basalt, these comfortable and conve-nient eco-friendly apartments are set on the water's edge. Guests can take advantage of a saltwater pool, and the Atlantic Ocean and Pico mountain views never cease to please.

Casa Hintze Ribeiro
MAP U2 ▪ Rua Hintze Ribeiro 62, Ponta Delgada, São Miguel ▪ (296) 304 340 ▪ www. casahintzeribeiro.com ▪ €€€
Named after the famous Portuguese politician Ernesto Hintze Ribeiro (1849–1907), this smart, design-led hotel bears the hallmarks of interior designer Nini Andrade Silva. The one-bedroom apartments feature kitchenettes and some have city-view terraces.

Octant Furnas Hotel
MAP E5 ▪ Avenida Dr Manuel de Arriaga, Furnas, São Miguel ▪ (296) 249 200 ▪ www.furnas. octanthotels.com ▪ €€€
Earthy tones, lots of dark wood and communal areas embellished with plants – this Zen-like retreat is designed around an attractive spa that offers a thermal pool, massage, reflexology and a range of treatments and therapies. The À Terra restaurant is noted for its healthy menu.

Furnas Lake Forest Living
MAP E6 ▪ Estrada Regional do Sul, Lagoa das Furnas, Furnas, São Miguel ▪ (296) 584 107 ▪ www.furnaslake.com ▪ €€€
These villas follow a minimalist Scandinavian style, inspired by local rustic granaries. The hotel is ideally placed for exploring the surrounding area, although a vehicle is recommended. Guests can sign up for outdoor activities. Breakfast can be served in the apartments.

Pocinho Bay
MAP L2 ▪ Pocinho, Candelária, Pico ▪ (292) 629 135 ▪ www.pocinho bay.com ▪ €€€
Located near Pico's UNESCO-listed vineyards *(see pp32–3)*, this charming retreat melds innovative interior design with a traditional home-style ambience. Each room is individually styled, and the views across the channel to Faial are beautiful.

Quinta do Mar

MAP C6 ■ Rua da Portela 43, Caloura, Água de Pau, São Miguel ■ (296) 913 990 ■ www.quintadomar-caloura.com ■ €€€
This stylish bolthole has been imaginatively fashioned out of a former winery. Amid tranquil gardens overlooking the sea, the en-suite rooms are set around an open-air swimming pool. Breakfast and snacks are served in the garden pavilion.

Budget Hotels

A Casa do Lado

MAP T2 ■ Rua D. Pedro IV 23, Horta, Faial ■ (292) 700 351 ■ www.acasadolado.com ■ €
Dario and Vanessa, the couple who run this traditionally styled guesthouse, encourage guests to lower the hotel's carbon footprint. Rooms are modest and have private bathrooms.

Guest House Malheiros Serpa

MAP R5 ■ Casa de Hóspedes, Malheiros Serpa, Rua do Hospital 8, Santa Cruz das Flores, Flores ■ (292) 592 201 ■ www.malheiros.net ■ €
A dozen furnished rooms – a mixture of double and singles – are available at this centrally located guesthouse, with rooms featuring en-suite bathrooms. Amenities include a fully equipped kitchen.

Hotel Branco

MAP P5 ■ Estrada 25 de Abril 2, Praia da Vitória, Terceira ■ (295) 513 459 ■ www.residencial-branco.com ■ €
This spruce guesthouse sits in a quiet corner of the town, but is within walking distance of the beach. All rooms have cable TVs and private bathrooms.

In53 Guest House

MAP U2 ■ Rua João Francisco Cabral 53, Ponta Delgada, São Miguel ■ (919) 801 999 ■ www.in53guesthouse.com ■ €
Pinewood flooring, patterned fabrics and an elegant, home-style ambience characterize this guesthouse. Two rooms, one of them furnished with bunk beds, allow for a maximum of four guests at a time. There's also access to a kitchen, bathrooms and lounge.

The Nook

MAP U1 ■ Travessa do Pedro Homem 2, Ponta Delgada, São Miguel ■ (967) 578 059 ■ www.thenookhostel.com ■ €
A brilliant example of how the Azores' burgeoning hostel sector is appealing to budget travellers with hotel-grade properties, this contemporary place close to the town centre offers a choice between shared and private rooms. Some of the rooms require a minimum two-night stay. There is a fully equipped kitchen, laundry service and lockers.

Residencial Bela Vista

MAP N3 ■ Avenida Marginal 1, Lajes do Pico, Pico ■ (962) 413 409 ■ www.lajesbelavista.com ■ €€€
Doubles, singles, triples and studios are quickly snapped up here over the summer. The lovely one-bedroom self-catering apartment is a delight to stay in. This is an ideal location for joining a whale-watching excursion or for exploring the island's eastern tip.

Hotel Soares Neto

MAP N1 ■ Rua Conselheiro Dr José Pereira 12, Velas, São Jorge ■ (295) 412 403 ■ www.hotelsoaresneto.com ■ €
The first accommodation option at which you arrive after stepping off the ferry, this simple hotel has been smartly refurbished. They can arrange airport shuttles and bicycle hire. There is a lovely rooftop pool too.

Hotel Santa Cruz

MAP J5 ■ Largo Barão de Guadalupe 9, Santa Cruz da Graciosa, Graciosa ■ (295) 712 345 ■ www.santacruzhotel.pt ■ €
Located on a terrace of traditional whitewashed townhouses, this guesthouse has 18 rooms with bathrooms and TVs. It is only 100 m (109 yards) from the sea, and a short walk from town.

Hotel São Miguel

MAP U2 ■ Rua Dr Bruno Tavares Carreiro 28, Ponta Delgada, São Miguel ■ (296) 286 086 ■ www.hotelsaomiguel.pt ■ €
There are 20 modest rooms with private bathrooms and cable TVs at this pleasant guesthouse situated in the historic downtown area. A continental breakfast is included in the rate.

For a key to hotel price categories see p112

General Index

Page numbers in **bold** refer to main entries

A

Absolutists 36–7
Accommodation 111, 112–17
Adega e Cooperativa Agrícola da Ilha Graciosa 81
Air travel 106, 107
Algar do Carvão (Terceira) 11, **30–31**, 42, 77
Ambulances 108
Angra do Heroísmo (Terceira) 10, **20–21**, 77, 79
Aquário de Porto Pim (Horta) 6, 27, 90
Arquipélago-Centro de Artes Contemporâneas (Ribeira Grande) 70
Arriaga, Manuel de 26, 37
Arruda Açores Pineapple Plantation (Ponta Delgada) 12
Arts and crafts 60–61
Associação de Artesãos da Ilha Graciosa 81
Associação de Criadores e Amigos do Burro Anão da Ilha Graciosa 81
Azores Wine Company 33
Azul, Lagoa (São Miguel) 14, 43, 67

B

B&Bs 115
Baía da Praia (Santa Maria) 46
Baía de São Lourenço (Santa Maria) 69, 72
Ballooning 51
Banco Dom João de Castro 25
Banco Dollabarat 25
Banco Princesa Alice 25
Banks 109
Bars 57
   São Jorge, Pico and Faial Islands 96
   São Miguel and Santa Maria Islands 74
   Terceira and Graciosa Islands 84
Basalt jewellery 60–61
Bazán, Álvaro de 36
Beaches 45
Birds 50, 52–3
   Centro de Reabilitação de Aves Selvagens do Corvo (Corvo) 102

Birds (cont.)
   Flores and Corvo Islands 100, 102
   São Miguel and Santa Maria Islands 73
   Terceira and Graciosa Islands 83
Biscoitos (Terceira) 44, 78
Boats
   arriving in the Azores 106, 107
   excursions to Corvo 102
   Flores boat tours 102
   Horta (Faial) 26, 27
   Oceaneye (Faial) 6, 94
   sailing 51, 73, 95
Boca do Algar do Carvão 30
Bola Gasosa (Algar do Carvão) 30
Breads, cakes and sweets 59, 61
Budget hotels 117
Buses 106–7

C

Cables, transatlantic 90
Cabral, Berta 37
Cabral, Gonçalo Velho 39, 69
Cafés 57
   São Jorge, Pico and Faial Islands 96
   São Miguel and Santa Maria Islands 74
   Terceira and Graciosa Islands 84
Cakes 59
Caldeira (Faial) 47, 91
Caldeira das Furnas (São Miguel) 18
Caldeira das Sete Cidades (São Miguel) 6, 10, **14–15**
Caldeira Guilherme Moniz (Algar do Carvão) 30
Caldeirão (Corvo) 43, 47, 100
Caldeira Velha (São Miguel) 44
Caldeirinhas (São Jorge) 7, 4
Calheta (São Jorge) 7, 45, 92
Calheta do Nesquim Trail (Pico) 93
Caloura (São Miguel) 70
Canário, Lagoa do (São Miguel) 15, 46
Caneiro dos Meros 25
Canoeing 50

Canto, José and Maria do 18
Canyoning 51
   Flores and Corvo Islands 102
   São Miguel and Santa Maria Islands 73
Capela de Nossa Senhora dos Anjos (Santa Maria) 39, 69, 72
Capelinhos (Faial) 6, 8–9, 11, **28–9**, 37, 42, 47, 91
Capelo–Capelinhos Trail 29
Capitão, Lagoa do (Pico) 91
Carapacho (Graciosa) 45
Carlos, King Dom 14
Cars 107
Casa de Artesanato Nunes (São Jorge) 92
Casa dos Dabney (Horta) 6, 26, 40, 41, 90
Casa Museu João Tomáz Bettencourt (Graciosa) 81
Casa-Museu Manuel de Arriaga (Horta) 26
Casa do Parque de São Jorge (São Jorge) 92
Cascading 102
Cascata da Ribeira Grande (Flores) 99
Castles
   Fortaleza de São João Baptista (Angra do Heroísmo) 21, 79
   Forte de São Brás (Santa Maria) 13, 72
"Cathedral" (Algar do Carvão) 31
Cathedrals
   Santíssimo Salvador da Sé (Angra do Heroísmo) 20
   see also Churches and chapels
Caves
   Algar do Carvão (Terceira) 11, **30–31**, 42
   Furna do Enxofre (Graciosa) 42, 78
   Gruta das Torres (Pico) 90, 91
   Gruta do Carvão (São Miguel) 6, 12
   Gruta dos Enxaréus (Flores) 24, 99
   Gruta e Ilhéu Negro (Faial) 25
   Grutas do Algar do Montoso (São Jorge) 7, 92

Caves (cont.)
  Miradouro da Boca do
    Inferno (São Miguel) 15
  Os Montanheiros
    (Terceira) 80
  São Jorge, Pico and
    Faial Islands 95
  Terceira and Graciosa
    Islands 83
Centro de Artesanato do
  Capelo (Faial) 6, 94
Centro de Interpretação
  Ambiental Dalberto
  (Santa Maria) 72
Centro de Interpretação
  Ambiental do Boqueirão
  (Flores) 100
Centro de Interpretação
  Ambiental e Cultural
  (Corvo) 101
Centro de Interpretação da
  Paisagem da Cultura da
  Vinha da Ilha do Pico 7, 33
Centro de Interpretação do
  Vulcão dos Capelinhos
  (Faial) 6, 29
Centro de Monitorização e
  Investigação das Furnas
  (São Miguel) 19
Centro de Reabilitação de
  Aves Selvagens do Corvo
  (Corvo) 102
Ceramics 60, 61
Cheeses 7, 92, 102
Churches and chapels
  39–9
  Capela de Nossa
    Senhora dos Anjos
    (Santa Maria) 39, 69, 72
  Convento e Santuário de
    Nossa Senhora da
    Esperança (Ponta
    Delgada) 13, 39
  Convento de São Gonçalo
    (Angra do Heroísmo)
    39, 79
  Ermida da Nossa
    Senhora da Ajuda
    (Graciosa) 39
  Ermida de Nossa
    Senhora das Vitórias
    (São Miguel) 18
  Igreja da Misericórdia
    (Angra do Heroísmo)
    20, 38
  Igreja de Nossa Senhora
    da Purificação (Santo
    Espírito) 38, 69
  Igreja de Santa Bárbara
    (São Jorge) 7, 38, 89
  Igreja de São Boaventura
    (Flores) 38–9
  Igreja de São Salvador
    (Horta) 27, 39

Churches and chapels
  (cont.)
  Igreja do Colégio (Ponta
    Delgada) 13, 38
  Igreja Matriz de São
    Sebastião (Ponta
    Delgada) 12, 34–5
  see also Cathedrals
Cinco Ribeiras (Terceira)
  80
Circuito das Furnas de
  Enxofre (Terceira) 80
Climbing 51, 95
Coasteering 51
Columbus, Christopher
  39, 69, 72
Complexo Monte de Guia
  (Faial) 90
Congro, Lagoa do (São
  Miguel) 70
Consulates 108, 109
Convents
  Convento de São
    Francisco (Angra do
    Heroísmo) 79
  Convento de São Gonçalo
    (Angra do Heroísmo)
    20, 39, 79
  Convento e Santuário de
    Nossa Senhora da
    Esperanca (Ponta
    Delgada) 13, 39
  Cooperativa de Artesanato
    Nossa Senhora da
    Encarnação (São Jorge)
    92
  Cooperativa Vitivinícola
    da Ilha do (Pico) 32, 93
  Correia, Natália 37
  Corvo see Flores and Corvo
    Islands
  Cozida das Furnas (São
    Miguel) 19
  Crafts 60–61
  Credit cards 109
  Criação Velha (Pico) 44
  Crime 108
  Cruise ships 106, 107
  Currency 109
  Customs and Immigration
    108, 109
  Cycling 51
    São Jorge, Pico and Faial
      Islands 95
    São Miguel and Santa
      Maria Islands 73

D

Dabney, John Bass 37,
  90
Dabney family 26, 40, 41
Deserto Vermelho dos
  Açores (Santa Maria) 43,
  69

Diving 11, **24–5**, 50
  Flores and Corvo Islands
    102
  São Jorge, Pico and Faial
    Islands 95
  São Miguel and Santa
    Maria Islands 73
  Terceira and Graciosa
    Islands 83
Doctors 108
Dolls, maize husk 61
Dolphins 10, **16–17**
  São Jorge, Pico and Faial
    Islands 95
  Terceira and Graciosa
    Islands 83
Dori (São Miguel) 24
Doze Ribeiras (Terceira) 80

E

Earthquake (1980) 79
Edwin L Drake 24
Electrical appliances 110
Embassies 108, 109
Embroidery 61, 81
Emergency services 108
Ermida da Nossa Senhora
  da Ajuda (Graciosa) 39
Ermida de Nossa Senhora
  das Vitórias (São Miguel)
  18
Escola Regional de
  Artesanato (Pico) 93
Events 63

F

Fábrica da Baleia de Porto
  Pim (Horta) 27, 94
Fábrica de Chá Gorreana
  (São Miguel) 68
Faial see São Jorge, Pico
  and Faial Islands
Fajã da Caldeira de Santo
  Cristo (São Jorge) 89
Fajã dos Cubres (São
  Jorge) 43, 89
Fajã Grande (Flores) 47, 99,
  101
Farol da Punta dos
  Capelinhos 28
Ferries 106, 107
Festa da Nossa Senhora
  da Assunção (Santa
  Maria) 63
Festa da Senhora da Guia
  (Faial) 62
Festa da Senhora do Bom
  Caminho (Corvo) 63
Festa do Emigrante
  (Flores) 62
Festas do Espírito Santo
  62
Festas Sanjoaninas
  (Terceira) 62

Festival da Ilha Branca (Graciosa) 62
Festivals 62–3
Fig tree pith carvings 61
Filipe II, King of Spain 21, 36
Fire services 108
Fish scale art 60
Fishing 51
  Flores and Corvo Islands 102
  Terceira and Graciosa Islands 83
Flores and Corvo Islands **98–103**
  maps 98, 101
  outdoor activities 102
  restaurants 103
Flowering plants 53
Fogo, Lagoa do (São Miguel) 64–5, 68
Food and drink 54–5
  breads, cakes and sweets 59, 61
  cheeses 7, 92, 102
  souvenirs 61
  see also Restaurants
Forbes, Rose Dabney 41
Formação do Arquipélago dos Açores (Capelinhos) 28
Forte de São Brás (Ponta Delgada) 13, 72
Furna do Enxofre (Graciosa) 42, 78
Furnas, Lagoa das (São Miguel) 19, 42
Furnas do Enxofre (Terceira) 31
Furnas Valley (São Miguel) see Vale das Furnas
Furnas Village (São Miguel) 19

G
Galleries see Museums and galleries
Gardens see Parks and gardens
Geotourism 51, 95
Ginetes (São Miguel) 15
Golfing 51
  São Miguel and Santa Maria Islands 73
  Terceira and Graciosa Islands 83
Graciosa see Terceira and Graciosa Islands
Gruta das Torres (Pico) 90, 91
Gruta do Carvão (São Miguel) 6, 12
Gruta do Natal (Terceira) 80

Gruta dos Enxaréus (Flores) 24, 99
Gruta e Ilhéu Negro (Faial) 25
Grutas do Algar do Montoso (São Jorge) 7, 92

H
Health 108, 109
  see also Hot springs
Hickling, Thomas 37
Hiking see Walks and hikes
History 36–7
Horse riding 51
  São Jorge, Pico and Faial Islands 95
  São Miguel and Santa Maria Islands 73
  Terceira and Graciosa Islands 83
Horta (Faial) 6, 11, **26–7**, 94
Hospitals 108
Hot springs 44–5
  Caldeira das Furnas (São Miguel) 18
  Furnas do Enxofre (Terceira) 31
  Lagoa das Furnas (São Miguel) 42
  Piscina de Água – Parque Terra Nostra (São Miguel) 45
  Poca da Dona Beija (São Miguel) 19, 44
  Ponta da Ferraria (São Miguel) 44
  Termas do Carapacho (Graciosa) 45, 51, 79, 83
Hot Air Ballooning 51
Hotels 111, 112–17
  boutique hotels 116
  budget hotels 117
  contemporary hotels 114
  eco and nature hotels 113
  historic hotels 112–13
Huerter, Josse van 41

I
Igreja da Misericórdia (Angra do Heroísmo) 20, 38
Igreja de Nossa Senhora da Purificação (Santo Espírito) 38, 69
Igreja de Santa Bárbara (São Jorge) 7, 38, 89
Igreja de São Boaventura (Flores) 38–9
Igreja de São Salvador (Horta) 27, 39
Igreja Matriz de São Sebastião (Ponta Delgada) 12, 34–5

Igreja do Colégio (Ponta Delgada) 13, 38
Ilhéu da Balaia (Graciosa) 81
Ilhéu da Praia (Graciosa) 78–9
Ilhéu do Topo (São Jorge) 25, 92
Ilhéus das Formigas 24
Império da Caridade (Terceira) 80
Insurance 108
Internet 110

J
Jardim Botânico do Faial (Faial) 26, 94
Jardim Duque da Terceira (Angro do Heroísmo) 21, 79
Jardim e Palácio de Sant'Anna (Ponta Delgada) 12
Jet skiing 51
Jewellery 60–61

K
Kayaking 50, 95

L
Lacerda, Francisco de 37
Lacticorvo (Corvo) 102
Ladeira dos Moinhos (Pico) 47
Lagedo (Flores) 99
Lagoa do Capitão Trail (Pico) 7, 93
Lajedo (Flores) 47
Lagido (Pico) 33
Lajes do Pico (Pico) 7, 91, 93
Language, phrase book 126–8
Lapinhas 60
Liberals 36–7
Lighthouses
  Capelinhos (Faial) 91
  Farol dos Capelinhos (Faial) 28
  Ponta da Barca (Graciosa) 81
Liqueurs 55
Loja do Parque da Lagoa das Sete Cidades (São Miguel) 14
Lombega (Faial) 94
Luis, Ana 37
Lusitano, Vasco Pereira 41

M
Machado, Carlos 37
Madalena (Pico) 7, 93
Magazines 110
Maia, Ernesto Canto da 37
Maia (Santa Maria) 72

Maize husk dolls 61
Maps
  Azores highlights 10–11
  Caldeira das Sete
    Cidades (São Miguel)
    15
  churches and chapels 39
  exploring the Azores
    6–7
  Flores and Corvo Islands
    98, 101
  Horta (Faial) 27
  natural wonders 42
  Ponta Delgada (São
    Miguel) 13
  São Jorge, Pico and Faial
    Islands 88–9, 91
  São Miguel and Santa
    Maria Islands 66–7, 69
  Terceira and Graciosa
    Islands 76–7
  Vale das Furnas (São
    Miguel) 19
Marina da Horta (Horta)
  6, 26
Marine life 25
Melo, Manuel João 70
Miradouro Caldeira do
  Faial (Faial) 47
Miradouro Caldeirão
  (Corvo) 47
Miradouro da Fajã do
  Ouvidor (São Jorge) 47
Miradouro da Fajãzinha
  (Flores) 47
Miradouro da Boca do
  Inferno (São Miguel) 15
Miradouro da Macela
  (Santa Maria) 47
Miradouro da Santa Iria
  (São Miguel) 47
Miradouro da Vista do Rei
  (São Miguel) 6, 14, 47
Miradouro de São Miguel
  Arcanjo (Pico) 47
Miradouro do Monte da
  Guia (Horta) 47
Miradouro do Pico do Ferro
  (São Miguel) 19
Miradouro do Pico Timão
  (Graciosa) 47
Miradouro do Raminho
  (Terceira) 47
Mistérios de São João
  (Pico) 93
Mistérios Negros
  (Terceira) 80
Mobile phones 109
Moinho do Frade (Pico) 33
Moinhos de Vento
  (Graciosa) 81
Money 108–9
Montanha do Pico (Pico) 7,
  42, 46, 88–9, 95

Monte da Ajuda (Graciosa)
  81
Monte da Guia (Faial) 94
Morro de Castelo Branco
  (Faial) 94
Mosteiros (São Miguel) 15,
  46
Mountain biking 51, 95
Museums and galleries
  40–41
  Adega A Buraca 93
  Casa dos Dabney
    (Faial) 90
  Casa Museu João Tomáz
    Bettencourt (Graciosa)
    81
  Casa-Museu Manuel de
    Arriaga (Horta) 26
  Centro de Interpretação
    Ambiental do
    Boqueirão (Flores) 100
  Centro de Interpretação
    Ambiental e Cultural
    (Corvo) 101
  Centro de Interpretação
    Ambiental Dalberto
    (Santa Maria) 72
  Centro de Interpretação
    do Vulcão dos
    Capelinhos 6, 29
  Escola Regional de
    Artesanato (Pico) 93
  Fábrica da Baleia de
    Porto Pim (Horta) 27
  Museu Carlos Machado
    (Ponta Delgada) 13, 41
  Museu da Fábrica da
    Baleia do Boqueirão
    (Flores) 99
  Museu da Graciosa
    (Graciosa) 41, 81
  Museu da Horta (Faial)
    6, 26, 40, 41, 90
  Museu da Indústria
    Baleeira (Pico) 91, 93
  Museu das Flores
    (Flores) 40, 41, 100, 101
  Museu de Angra do
    Heroísmo (Terceira) 20,
    40, 41, 79
  Museu de Santa Maria
    (Santa Maria) 69, 72
  Museu de Scrimshaw
    (Horta) 26, 40–41
  Museu dos Baleeiros
    (Pico) 7, 41, 91
  Museu do Vinho dos
    Biscoitos (Terceira) 77
  Museu do Vinho (Pico) 7,
    32, 40, 41, 90
  Museu Militar dos Açores
    (São Miguel) 70
  Núcleo de Arte Sacra –
    Igreja do Colégio 41

N
Natural wonders 42–3
Naufrágio Terceirense
  (Graciosa) 25
Newspapers 110
Nordeste (São Miguel)
  70
Noronha, António José
  Severim de, Count of
  Vila Flor 37
Norte Grande (São Jorge)
  7, 46
Núcleo de Arte Sacra –
  Igreja do Colégio (Ponta
  Delgada) 40, 41

O
Observatório Microbiano
  dos Açores (São Miguel)
  19
Oceaneye (Faial) 6, 94
Oficina-Museu das
  Capelas (São Miguel) 70
Opening hours 110
Os Montanheiros (Terceira)
  80
Outdoor activities 50–51
  Flores and Corvo
    Islands 102
  São Jorge, Pico and Faial
    Islands 95
  São Miguel and Santa
    Maria Islands 73
  Terceira and Graciosa
    Islands 83
Outeiro da Memória (Angra
  do Heroísmo) 21, 79

P
Paisagem da Cultura da
  Vinha da Ilha do Pico
  (Pico) 11, **32–3**, 93
Palácio Bettencourt (Angra
  do Heroísmo) 20
Palácio dos Capitães
  Generais (Angra do
  Heroísmo) 20, 79
Paragliding 51
Parks and gardens
  Arruda Açores Pineapple
    Plantation (Ponta
    Delgada) 12
  Jardim Botânico do Faial
    (Faial) 6, 94
  Jardim Duque da
    Terceira (Angro do
    Heroísmo) 21, 79
  Jardim e Palácio de
    Sant'Anna (Ponta
    Delgada) 12
  Parque Terra Nostra
    (São Miguel) 18
  Parque Florestal do Capelo
    (Faial) 29, 94

Parque Florestal das Sete Fontes (São Jorge) 92
Passports 108, 109
Pedreira do Campo (Santa Maria) 72
Pedro IV, King Dom 21
Personal security 108, 109
Phrase book 126–7
Pico see São Jorge, Pico and Faial Islands
Pico Alto (Santa Maria) 72
Pineapple 12
  Arruda Açores Pineapple Plantation (Ponta Delgada) 12
Piscina de Água – Parque Terra Nostra (São Miguel) 45
Plants, flowering 53
Poca da Dona Beíja (São Miguel) 19, 44
Police 108, 109
Pombo, Dalberto 68
Ponta da Barca (Graciosa) 81
Ponta da Espalamaca (Faial) 94
Ponta da Ferraria (São Miguel) 44
Ponta das Contendas (Terceira) 80
Ponta Delgada (Flores) 47, 99
Ponta Delgada (São Miguel) 6, 10, **12–13**, 67
Ponta do Escalvado (São Miguel) 15
Ponta do Raminho (Terceira) 46
Portas de Cidade (Ponta Delgada) 12
Portas do Mar (Ponta Delgada) 13
Postal services 110
Praia (Graciosa) 45, 46, 81
Praia (Santa Maria) 69, 72
Praia da Angro do Heroísmo (Terceira) 45
Praia da Formosa (Santa Maria) 45, 68–9
Praia da Vitória (Terceira) 45, 78
Praia de Água d'Alto (São Miguel) 45
Praia de Santa Bárbara (São Miguel) 45
Praia do Almoxarife (Faial) 45, 94
Praia do Pópulo (São Miguel) 45
Praia do Porto Pim (Faial) 45
Praia Fajã Grande (Flores) 45

R
Rabo do Asno (São Miguel) 15
Radio 110
Rappelling 51
Restaurants 56–7, 111
  Flores and Corvo Islands 103
  São Jorge, Pico and Faial Islands 97
  São Miguel and Santa Maria Islands 75
  Terceira and Graciosa Islands 85
  see also Food and drink
Ribeira Grande (São Miguel) 67
Ribeira de Maloás (Santa Maria) 72
Rilheiras (Pico) 32
Rocha dos Bordões (Flores) 43, 101
Rola-Pipas (Pico) 33
Romaria de Santo Cristo (São Jorge) 63
Rua Direita (Angra do Heroísmo) 20

S
Sabrina (volcanic island) 14
Safety 108, 109
Sailing 51
  São Jorge, Pico and Faial Islands 95
  São Miguel and Santa Maria Islands 73
Sala Holograma (Capelinhos) 28
Santa Cruz das Flores (Flores) 44
Santa Cruz da Graciosa (Graciosa) 78
Santa Maria see São Miguel and Santa Maria Islands
Santana (Pico) 33
Santíssimo Salvador da Sé (Angra do Heroísmo) 20
Santo Espírito (Santa Maria) 69
São Jorge, Pico and Faial Islands 6–7, **88–97**
  attractions: Pico 93
  The best of the rest: São Jorge 92
  cafés and bars 96
  a day exploring Pico 91
  maps 88–9, 91
  outdoor activities 95
  restaurants 97
  sights: Faial 94

São Miguel and Santa Maria Islands 6, **66–75**
  The best of the rest: São Miguel 70
  cafés and bars 74
  exploring Santa Maria Island 69
  maps 66–7, 69
  outdoor activities 73
  restaurants 75
  shops: São Miguel 71
  sights: Santa Maria 72
São Roque do Pico (Pico) 47
Scrimshaw 60
  Museu das Flores (Flores) 100
  Museu de Scrimshaw (Horta) 26, 40–41
Semana dos Baleeiros (Pico) 63
Senhor Santo Cristo dos Milagres (São Miguel) 62
Serra Branca (Graciosa) 46
Serra da Tronqueira (São Miguel) 70
Serra de Santa Bárbara (Terceira) 77
Serra do Cume (Terceira) 80
Serra do Topo (São Jorge) 89
Serreta (Terceira) 46, 80
Sete Cidades (São Miguel) 15, 46
Sete Cidades, Caldeira das (São Miguel) 43, 67
Sete Lagoas (Flores) 101
Shopping 58–9, 111
  opening hours 110
  São Miguel 71
  Terceira and Graciosa Islands 82
Shows and events 63
Silveira Rosa, Euclides da 26
Sinagoga de Ponta Delgada (Ponta Delgada) 70
Snorkelling 50
Sousa Pinto, José Júlio 90
Souvenirs 61
Sports 50–51
  São Jorge, Pico and Faial Islands 95
  São Miguel and Santa Maria Islands 73
  Terceira and Graciosa Islands 83
Squid 93
Stalactites 30

Stand-up Paddleboarding (SUP) 51, 83
Surfing 50, 73
Swimming pools, natural 44–5

T

Tanque do – Atalho (Graciosa) 81
Taxis 107
Tea 61, 68
Telephones 110
Television 110
Ten Volcanoes Trail 29
Terceira and Graciosa Islands **76–85**
  attractions: Graciosa 81
  The best of the rest: Terceira 80
  cafés and bars 84
  maps 76–7, 79
  outdoor activities 83
  restaurants 85
  shops 82
Terceirense 25
Termas do Carapacho (Graciosa) 45, 51, 79, 83
Thermal springs *see* Hot springs
Tidal wells (Pico) 33
Time zone 110
Topo (São Jorge) 92
Torre Sineira (Ponta Delgada) 70
Tourist information 110
Tours 102, 110–11
Transatlantic cables 90
Travel 106–7
Travel insurance 108
Travel safety advice 108, 109
Travellers' cheques 109
Travellers with specific needs 108–9
Trekking *see* Walks
Trips and tours 110–11

U

UNESCO Biosphere Reserves
  Corvo 43, 101
  fajãs (São Jorge) 43, 89
  Flores 43
  Ilhéu da Praia (Graciosa) 79
  Terceira 76
UNESCO World Heritage Sites
  Angra do Heroísmo (Terceira) 10, **20–21**, 37, 77
  Graciosa 42
  Paisagem da Cultura da Vinha da Ilha do Pico 11, **32–3**, 37, 91, 93

Uniqueijo (São Jorge) 7, 92
Urzelina (São Jorge) 92

V

Vaccinations 108
Vale das Furnas (São Miguel) 6, 10, **18–19**, 68
Varadouro (Faial) 45
Velas (São Jorge) 7, 92
Verde, Lagoa (São Miguel) 14, 67
Viewpoints 47
Vila do Corvo (Corvo) 47
Vila do Porto (Santa Maria) 46, 68
Vila Franca do Campo (São Miguel) 6, 70
Vineyards *see* Wines
Vinhas da Criação Velha Trail (Pico) 7, 33
Violas 60
Visas 108, 109
Visitor information 110
Vista do Rei (São Miguel) 15
Volcanoes
  Algar do Carvão (Terceira) 77
  Caldeira (Faial) 91
  Caldeira das Sete Cidades (São Miguel) 6, 10, **14–15**
  Caldeirão (Corvo) 43, 100
  Capelinhos (Faial) 6, **28–9**, 37, 42
  Centro de Interpretação do Vulcão dos Capelinhos (Faial) 6, 29
  Montanha do Pico (Pico) 7, 42
  see also Hot springs

W

Walks and hikes 46–7, 50
  Angra do Heroísmo (Terceira) 79
  Calheta do Nesquim Trail (Pico) 93
  Capelo–Capelinhos Trail 29
  Flores 99, 102
  Lagoa do Capitão Trail (Pico) 7, 93
  Lombega–Morro de Castelo Branco Trail (Faial) 94
  Mosteiros–Ponta do Escalvado–Ginetes-Rabo do Asno Trail (São Miguel) 15
  Rei–Sete Cidades Trail (São Miguel) 15
  Santana–Lagido Trail (Pico) 33

Walks and hikes (cont.)
  São Jorge 89, 95
  São Miguel and Santa Maria Islands 73
  Ten Volcanoes Trail (Capelinhos) 29
  Terceira and Graciosa Islands 83
  Vinhas da Criação Velha Trail (Pico) 7, 33
Water, drinking 108
Waterfalls
  cascading 102
  Cascata da Ribeira Grande (Flores) 99
Weather 110
Weaving 60
Whales
  Fábrica da Baleia de Porto Pim (Horta) 27, 94
  Museu da Indústria Baleeira (Pico) 93
  Museu da Fábrica da Baleia do Boquerão (Flores) 94
  Museu de Scrimshaw (Horta) 26, 40–41
  Museu dos Baleeiros (Pico) 7, 41, 91
  São Jorge, Pico and Faial Islands 95
  scrimshaw 60
  Terceira and Graciosa Islands 83
  whale-watching 10, **16–17**, 50, 73
  whaling ban 37
Wildlife
  Algar do Carvão (Terceira) 31
  Lagoa das Furnas (São Miguel) 19
  marine life 25
  Oceaneye (Faial) 6, 94
  see also Birds; Whales
Windmills 81, 94
Wines 55, 61
  Adega e Cooperativa Agrícola da Ilha Graciosa 81
  Centro de Interpretação da Paisagem da Cultura da Vinha da Ilha do Pico 7, 33
  Cooperativa Vitivinícola da Ilha do (Pico) 32, 93
  Museu do Vinho (Pico) 7, 32, 40, 41, 90
  Museu do Vinho dos Biscoitos (Terceira) 77
  vineyard tours 95
World War II 37

Acknowledgments

This edition updated by

Contributor Keith Drew
Senior Editor Alison McGill
Senior Designer Stuti Tiwari
Project Editor Parnika Bagla
Project Art Editor Ankita Sharma
Editors Chhavi Nagpal, Anuroop Sanwalia, Mark Silas
Picture Research Administrator Vagisha Pushp
Picture Research Manager Taiyaba Khatoon
Publishing Assistant Halima Mohammed
Jacket Designer Jordan Lambley
Senior Cartographer Mohammed Hassan
Cartography Manager Suresh Kumar
DTP Designer Rohit Rojal
Senior Production Editor Jason Little
Production Controller Kariss Ainsworth
Deputy Managing Editor Beverly Smart
Managing Editors Shikha Kulkarni, Hollie Teague
Managing Art Editor Sarah Snelling
Senior Managing Art Editor Priyanka Thakur
Art Director Maxine Pedliham
Publishing Director Georgina Dee

DK would like to thank the following for their contribution to the previous editions: Paul Bernhardt, Hilary Bird, Mark Harding, Christine Stroyan

The publisher would like to thank the following for their kind permission to reproduce their photographs:

(**Key:** a-above; b-below/bottom; c-centre; f-far; l-left; r-right; t-top)

123RF.com: Steven Phraner 66ca; Rui Santos 19tl; Martin Schlecht 69tl.
4Corners: Günter Gräfenhain 22-3.
akg-images: Album/sfgp 36b.
Alamy Stock Photo: Mauricio Abreu 62b; age fotostock/Juan Carlos Muñoz 6tr; All Canada Photos/Glenn Bartley 102cl; Art Collection 3 36ca; Art Directors & TRIP/Stephen Coyne 78bc; Gaspar Avila 43br, 54br, 61cl, 62tc; Paul Bernhardt 75cra; blickwinkel/McPHOTO/DEB 2tl, 8-9; Cro Magnon 93t; Danita Delimont/Walter Bibikow 74tr; Carlos Duarte 83b; Nuno Fonseca 33cb, 40t, 53tr; Oliver Hoffmann 18bl; imageBROKER/Frauke Scholz 80b, 86-7, /Michael Weberberger 17tr; Brian Jannsen 31tl; Lukasz Janyst 10ca, 98cla; LatitudeStock/Stephen Coyne 4cra; LOOK Die Bildagentur der Fotografen GmbH / Holger Leue 4t, /Thomas Stankiewicz 89tr, 94cr, 102tr; Marshall Ikonography 4b; mauritius images GmbH/P. Kaczynski 92cla; National Geographic Creative/Mauricio Handler 10cb; Nature Picture Library/Wild Wonders of Europe/Lundgren 25cl; parkerphotography 12-3, 39c; Anthony Pierce 16-7; REDA & CO srl/Marco Simonini 26-7, 31tl; Dirk Renckhoff 4cl, 28br, 92br; Manuel Ribeiro 47tr; robertharding/Ken Gillham 47cr; Pere Sanz 3tl, 3tr, 64-5, 104-5; Kevin Schafer 27tl; Gonçalo Silva 68cla; Marco Simonini 30cl; Stefan Sollfors 58tc, 71bl; Charles Stirling (Diving) 24bl; SuperStock/ David Forman 21tr; TNT Magazine 77cr; Jorge Tutor 45cla, 99tr; WWpics/Kike Calvo 26crb; WaterFrame 11tr, 25tc, 25clb, 48-9; Westend61 GmbH/Lisa und Wilfried Bahnmäller 95bl.

Arco 8: 75tr.
Rafael Armada: 52t, 52bc.
AWL Images: Mauricio Abreu 11cra; Karol Kozlowski 28-9.
Azores Golf Islands: Aidan Bradley 73crb.
Paul Bernhardt: 14br, 20ca, 20br, 32clb, 33t, 33br, 40c, 41cl, 41br, 38tl, 54b, 55tr, 55cl, 55b, 58bl, 59tr, 59cla, 60tc, 60bl, 61br, 70c, 71cr, 75bl, 81clb, 82cla, 96cla.
Birou Bar: 84bl.
Casa do Rei: 103clb.
Cella Bar: Fernando Guerra SG 97br.
Dreamstime.com: Billkret 11tl; Bizyyes 4cla; Edomor 29cr; Eyewave 7cla, 19crb, 20-1, 44tl, 76cla; Gadzius 32-3; Gezafarkas 70tr; H368k742 30br, 68b, 101bl; Hdamke 7tr, 90-1; Lukasz Janyst 1; Karnizz 12br; Klicaqui 46bl, 63cl; Lovasz 29tr; Lsantilli 46t; Mirisek 45br; Paop 2tr, 15cr, 34-5, 55tl; Perszing1982 18-9, 99b; ruigsantos 43t; Rvdschoot 88cl; Snogueira 10br.
Espaço Talassa: 50b.
FLPA: Malcolm Schuyl 53clb.
Getty Images: 37cla; Mauricio Abreu 62b; 78cl, 78-9, 95tr, 100t; Bruce Yuanyue Bi 6cl; Ana del Castillo 12cla; Richard Cummins 27cr; Danita Delimont 100clb; Getty Images Sport/Handout 63tr; Phil Inglis 51tr; Valter Jacinto 10clb; Justin Hart Marine Life Photography and Art 4clb; Wolfgang Kaehler 72cla, 81tc; LOOK-foto/Thomas Stankiewicz 42cla,44b; Frank Lukasseck 15tl; Scott Portelli 17c; Frauke Scholz 31br; Gerard Soury 16cr; ullstein bild 37tr; Westend61 67tr.
Getty Images/iStock: opsalka 14-15.
Graciosa Resort: 85cl.
Museu da Horta: 26bl.

Museu do Pico: 11bl.

Photoshot: Franco Banfi 38b; LOOK/Reinhard Dirscherl 50tl, /Thomas Stankiewicz 11crb; NHPA/Franco Banfi 24r.

Restaurant Anfiteatro: 54tr, 54c.

Gonçalo M. Rosa: 73tc.

SuperStock: age fotostock /David Muscroft 10cra, /Juan Carlos Muñoz 90tr; Mauritius/ Obert 30cla.

WestCanyon Turismo Aventura: 51cl.

Cover
Front and spine: **Dreamstime.com:** Lukasz Janyst.

Back: **Alamy Stock Photo:** National Geographic Image Collection tl; **Dreamstime.com:** Lukasz Janyst b; **Getty Images/iStock:** sack tr, sack crb, sack cla.

Pull Out Map Cover
Dreamstime.com: Lukasz Janyst.

All other images © Dorling Kindersley

For further information see:
www.dkimages.com

Maps in this book are derived from © OpenStreetMap contributors, see www.openstreetmap.org/copyright for further details.

Penguin Random House

First Edition 2017

Published in Great Britain by Dorling Kindersley Limited
DK, One Embassy Gardens, 8 Viaduct Gardens, London SW11 7BW, UK

The authorised representative in the EEA is Dorling Kindersley Verlag GmbH. Arnulfstr. 124, 80636 Munich, Germany

Published in the United States by DK Publishing, 1745 Broadway, 20th Floor, New York, NY 10019, USA

ISSN 1479-344X

ISBN 978-0-2415-6899-6

Printed and bound in Malaysia

www.dk.com

*As a guide to abbreviations in visitor information blocks: **Adm** = admission charge; **D** = dinner; **L** = lunch.*

MIX
Paper from
responsible sources
FSC™ C018179

Phrase Book

In an Emergency

Help!	Socorro!	soo-koh-roo!
Stop!	Pára!	pahr'!
Call a doctor!	Chame um médico!	shahm' ooñ meh-dee-koo!
Call an ambulance!	Chame uma ambulância!	shahm' oo-muh añ-boo-lañ-see-uh!
Call the police!	Chame a polícia!	shahm' uh poo-lee-see-uh!
Call the fire brigade!	Chame os bombeiros!	shahm' oosh' bom-bay-roosh!
Where is the nearest telephone?	Há um telefone aqui perto?	ah ooñ te-le-fon' uh-kee pehr-too?
Where is the nearest hospital?	Onde é o hospital mais próximo?	ond' eh oo ohsh-pee-tahl' mysh pro-see-moo?

Communication Essentials

Yes	Sim	seeñ
No	Não	nowñ
Please	Por favor/ Se faz favor	poor fuh-vor se-fash fuh-vor
Thank you	Obrigado/da	o-bree-gah-doo/duh
Excuse me	Desculpe	dish-koolp'
Hello	Olá	oh-lah
Goodbye	Adeus	a-deh-oosh
Good morning	Bom dia	boñ dee-uh
Good afternoon	Boa tarde	boh-uh tard'
Good night	Boa noite	boh-uh noyt'
Yesterday	Ontem	oñ-tayñ
Today	Hoje	ohj'
Tomorrow	Amanhã	ah-mañ yañ
Here	Aqui	uh-kee
There	Ali	uh-lee
What?	O quê?	oo keh?
Which?	Qual?	kwahl'?
When?	Quando?	kwañ-doo?
Why?	Porquê?	poor-keh?
Where?	Onde?	oñd'?

Useful Phrases

How are you?	Como está?	koh-moo shtah?
Very well, thank you	Bem, obrigado/da	bayñ, o-bree gah-doo/duh
Pleased to meet you	Encantado/a	eñ-kañ-tah-doo/duh
See you soon	Até logo	uh-teh loh-goo
That's fine	Está bem	shtah bayñ
Where is/are…?	Onde está/ estão…?	ond' shtah/ shtowñ…?
How far is it to…?	A que distância fica…?	uh kee dish-tañ-see-uh fee-kuh…?
Which way to…?	Como se vai para…?	koh-moo seh vy puh-ruh…?
Do you speak English?	Fala Inglês?	fah-luh eeñ-glehsh?
I don't understand	Não compreendo	nowñ kom-pree-eñ-doo
I'm sorry	Desculpe	dish-koolp'
Could you speak more slowly, please?	Pode falar mais devagar, por favor?	pohd' fuh-lar mysh d'-va-gar, poor fah-vor?

Useful Words

big	grande	grañd'
small	pequeno	pe-keh-noo
hot	quente	keñt'
cold	frio	free-oo
good	bom	boñ
bad	mau	mah-oo
enough	bastante	bash-tañt'
well	bem	bayñ
open	aberto	a-behr-too
closed	fechado	fe-shah-doo
left	esquerda	shkehr-duh
right	direita	dee-ray-tuh
straight on	em frente	ayñ freñt'
near	perto	pehr-too
far	longe	loñj'
up	suba	soo-bah
down	desça	deh-shuh
early	cedo	seh-doo
late	tarde	tard'
entrance	entrada	eñ-trah-duh
exit	saída	sa-ee-duh
toilets	casa de banho	kah-zuh d' bañ-yoo
more	mais	mysh
less	menos	meh-noosh

Making a Telephone Call

I would like to place an international call	Queria fazer uma chamada internacional	kree-uh fuh-zehr oo-muh sha-mah-duh in-ter-na-see-oo-nahl'
a local call	uma chamada local	oo-muh sha-mah-duh loo-kahl'
Can I leave a message?	Posso deixar uma mensagem?	poh-soo day-shar oo-muh meñ-sah-jayñ?

Shopping

How much does this cost?	Quanto custa isto?	kwañ-too koosh-tuh eesh-too?
I would like…	Queria…	kree-uh…
I'm just looking	Estou só a ver obrigado/a	shtoh soh uh vehr o-bree-gah-doo/uh
Do you take credit cards?	Aceita cartões de crédito?	uh-say-tuh kar-toinsh de kreh-dee-too?
What time do you open?	A que horas abre?	uh kee oh-rash ah-bre?
What time do you close?	A que horas fecha?	uh kee oh-rash fay-shuh?
this one	este	ehst'
that one	esse	ehss'
expensive	caro	kah-roo
cheap	barato	buh-rah-too
size (clothes/ shoes)	número	noom'-roo
white	branco	brañ-koo
black	preto	preh-too
red	vermelho	ver-melh-yoo
yellow	amarelo	uh-muh-reh-loo
green	verde	vehrd'
blue	azul	uh-zool'

Types of Shop

antique shop	loja de antiguidades	loh-juh de añ-tee-gwee-dahd'sh
bakery	padaria	pah-duh-ree-uh
bank	banco	bañ-koo
bookshop	livraria	lee-vruh-ree-uh
butcher	talho	tah-lyoo
cake shop	pastelaria	pash-te-luh-ree-uh
chemist	farmácia	far-mah-see-uh
fishmonger	peixaria	pay-shuh-ree-uh
hairdresser	cabeleireiro	kab'-lay-ray-roo
market	mercado	mehr-kah-doo
newsagent	quiosque	kee-yohsk'
post office	correios	koo-ray-oosh
shoe shop	sapataria	suh-puh-tuh-ree-uh
supermarket	supermercado	soo-pehr-mer-kah-doo
tobacconist	tabacaria	tuh-buh-kuh-ree-uh
travel agency	agência de viagens	uh-jen-see-uh de vee-ah-jayñsh

Sightseeing

cathedral	sé	seh
church	igreja	ee-gray-juh
garden	jardim	jar-deeñ
library	biblioteca	bee-blee-oo-teh-kuh
museum	museu	moo-zeh-oo
tourist information	posto de turismo	posh-too d' too-reesh-moo
closed for holidays	fechado para férias	fe-sha-doo puh-ruh feh-ree-ash
bus station	estação de autocarros	shta-sowñ d' oh-too-kah-roosh
railway station	estação de comboios	shta-sowñ d' koñ-boy-oosh
painted ceramic tile	azulejo	uh-zoo-lay-joo
Manueline (late Gothic architectural style)	manuelino	ma-noo-el-ee-oo

Staying in a Hotel

Do you have a vacant room?	Tem um quarto livre?	tayñ ooñ kwar-too leevr'?
room with a bath	um quarto com casa de banho	ooñ kwar-too koñ kah-zuh d' bañ-yoo
shower	duche	doosh
single room	quarto individual	kwar-too een-dee-vee-doo-ahl'
double room	quarto de casal	kwar-too d' kuh-zhal'
twin room	quarto com duas camas	kwar-too koñ doo-ash kah-mash
porter	porteiro	poor-tay-roo
key	chave	shahv'
I have a reservation	Tenho um quarto reservado	tayñ-yoo ooñ kwar-too re-ser-vah-doo

Eating Out

Have you got a table for…?	Tem uma mesa para…?	tayñ oo-muh meh-zuh puh-ruh?
I would like to reserve a table	Quero reservar uma mesa	keh-roo re-zehr-var oo-muh meh-zuh
The bill, please	A conta por favor/se faz favor	uh kohn-tuh poor fuh-vor/ se-fash fuh-vor
I am a vegetarian	Sou vegetariano/a	Soh ve-je-tuh-ree-ah-noo/uh
Waiter!	Por favor!/ Se faz favor!	poor fuh-vor/ se-fash fuh-vor!
the menu	a lista	uh leesh-tuh
fixed-price menu	a ementa turística	uh ee-mehñ-tuh too-reesh-tee-kuh
wine list	a lista de vinhos	uh leesh-tuh de veeñ-yoosh
glass	um copo	ooñ koh-poo
bottle	uma garrafa	oo-muh guh-rah-fuh
half-bottle	meia-garrafa	may-uh guh-rah-fuh
knife	uma faca	oo-mah fah-kuh
fork	um garfo	ooñ gar-foo
spoon	uma colher	oo-muh kool-yair
plate	um prato	ooñ prah-too
breakfast	pequeno-almoço	pe-keh-noo-ahl-moh-soo
lunch	almoço	ahl-moh-soo
dinner	jantar	jan-tar
cover	couvert	koo-vehr
starter	entrada	eñ-trah-duh
main course	prato principal	prah-too prin-see-pahl'
dish of the day	prato do dia	prah-too doo dee-uh
set dish	combinado	koñ-bee-nah-doo
half-portion	meia-dose	may-uh doh-se
dessert	sobremesa	soh-bre-meh-zuh
rare	mal passado	mahl' puh-sah-doo
medium	médio	meh-dee-oo
well done	bem passado	bayñ puh-sah-doo

Menu Decoder

abacate	uh-buh-kaht'	avocado
açorda	uh-sor-duh	bread-based stew (often seafood)
açúcar	uh-soo-kar	sugar
água mineral	ah-gwuh mee-ne-rahl'	mineral water
alho	ay-oo	garlic
alperce	ahl'-pehrce	apricot
amêijoas	uh-may-joo-ash	clams
ananás	uh-nuh-nahsh	pineapple
arroz	uh-rohsh	rice
assado	uh-sah-doo	baked
atum	uh-tooñ	tuna
aves	ah-vesh	poultry
azeite	uh-zayt'	olive oil
azeitonas	uh-zay-toh-nash	olives
bacalhau	buh-kuh-lyow	dried, salted cod
banana	buh-nah-nuh	banana
batatas	buh-tah-tash	potatoes
batatas fritas	buh-tah-tash free-tash	French fries

batido	*buh-**tee**-doo*	milkshake
bica	*bee-kuh*	espresso
bife	*beef*	steak
bolacha	*boo-**lah**-shuh*	biscuit
bolo	*boh-loo*	cake
borrego	*boo-**reh**-goo*	lamb
caça	*kah-ssuh*	game
café	*kuh-feh*	coffee
camarões	*kuh-muh-**roysh***	large prawns
caracóis	*kuh-ruh-**koysh***	snails
caranguejo	*kuh-rañ **gay**-yoo*	crabs
carne	*karn'*	meat
cataplana	*kuh-tuh-**plah**-nah*	sealed wok used to steam dishes
cebola	*se-**boh**-luh*	onion
cerveja	*sehr-**vay**-juh*	beer
chá	*shah*	tea
cherne	*shern'*	stone bass
chocolate	*shoh-koh-**laht'***	chocolate
chocos	*shoh-koosh*	cuttlefish
chouriço	*shoh-**ree**-soo*	red, spicy sausage
churrasco	*shoo-**rash**-coo*	on the spit
cogumelo	*koo-goo-**meh**-loo*	mushroom
cozido	*koo-**zee**-doo*	boiled
enguias	*eñ-**gee**-ash*	eels
fiambre	*fee-**añbr'***	ham
fígado	*fee-guh-doo*	liver
frango	*frañ-goo*	chicken
frito	*free-too*	fried
fruta	*froo-tuh*	fruit
gambas	*gañ-bash*	prawns
gelado	*je-**lah**-doo*	ice cream
gelo	*jeh-**loo***	ice
goraz	*goo-rash*	bream
grelhado	*grel-**yah**-doo*	grilled
iscas	*eesh-kash*	marinated liver
lagosta	*luh-**gohsh**-tuh*	lobster
laranja	*luh rañ-juh*	orange
leite	*layt'*	milk
limão	*lee-**mowñ***	lemon
limonada	*lee-moo-**nah**-duh*	lemonade
linguado	*leeñ-**gwah**-doo*	sole
lulas	*loo-lash*	squid
maçã	*muh-**sañ***	apple
manteiga	*mañ-**tay**-guh*	butter
marisco	*muh-**reesh**-koo*	seafood
meia-de-leite	*may-uh-d'**layt'***	white coffee
ostras	*osh-trash*	oysters
ovos	*oh-voosh*	eggs
pão	*powñ*	bread
pastel	*pash-**tehl'***	cake
pato	*pah-too*	duck
peixe	*paysh'*	fish
peixe-espada	*paysh'-**shpah**-duh*	scabbard fish
pimenta	*pee-**meñ**-tuh*	pepper
polvo	*pohl'-voo*	octopus
porco	*por-coo*	pork
queijo	*kay-joo*	cheese
sal	*sahl'*	salt
salada	*suh-**lah**-duh*	salad
salsichas	*sahl-**see**-shash*	sausages
sandes	*sañ-desh*	sandwich
sopa	*soh-puh*	soup
sumo	*soo-moo*	juice
tamboril	*tañ-boo-**ril'***	monkfish
tarte	*tart'*	pie/cake
tomate	*too-**maht'***	tomato
torrada	*too-**rah**-duh*	toast
tosta	*tohsh-tuh*	toasted sandwich
vinagre	*vee-**nah**-gre*	vinegar
vinho branco	*veeñ-yoo brañ-koo*	white wine
vinho tinto	*veeñ-yoo teeñ-too*	red wine
vitela	*vee-**teh**-luh*	veal

Numbers

0	zero	*zeh-roo*
1	um	*ooñ*
2	dois	*doysh*
3	três	*tresh*
4	quatro	*kwa-troo*
5	cinco	*seeñ-koo*
6	seis	*saysh*
7	sete	*set'*
8	oito	*oy-too*
9	nove	*nov'*
10	dez	*desh*
11	onze	*oñz'*
12	doze	*doz'*
13	treze	*trez'*
14	catorze	*ka-torz'*
15	quinze	*keeñz'*
16	dezasseis	*de-zuh-**saysh***
17	dezassete	*de-zuh-**set'***
18	dezoito	*de-**zoy**-too*
19	dezanove	*de-zuh-**nov'***
20	vinte	*veent'*
21	vinte e um	*veen-tee-**ooñ***
30	trinta	*treeñ-tuh*
40	quarenta	*kwa-**reñ**-tuh*
50	cinquenta	*seen-**kweñ**-tuh*
60	sessenta	*se-**señ**-tuh*
70	setenta	*se-**teñ**-tuh*
80	oitenta	*oy-**teñ**-tuh*
90	noventa	*noo-**veñ**-tuh*
100	cem	*sayñ*
101	cento e um	*señ-too-ee-**ooñ***
102	cento e dois	*señ-too-ee-**doysh***
200	duzentos	*doo-**zeñ**-toosh*
300	trezentos	*tre-**zeñ**-toosh*
400	quatrocentos	*kwa-troo-**señ**-toosh*
500	quinhentos	*kee-**nyeñ**-toosh*
600	seiscentos	*saysh-**señ**-toosh*
700	setecentos	*set'-**señ**-toosh*
800	oitocentos	*oy-too-**señ**-toosh*
900	novecentos	*nov'-**señ**-toosh*
1,000	mil	*meel'*

Time

one minute	um minuto	*ooñ mee-**noo**-too*
one hour	uma hora	*oo-muh **oh**-ruh*
half an hour	meia hora	*may-uh oh-ruh*
Monday	segunda-feira	*se-**goon**-duh-fay-ruh*
Tuesday	terça-feira	*ter-sa-**fay**-ruh*
Wednesday	quarta-feira	*kwar-ta-**fay**-ruh*
Thursday	quinta-feira	*keen-ta-**fay**-ruh*
Friday	sexta-feira	*say-shta-**fay**-ruh*
Saturday	sábado	*sah-ba-too*
Sunday	domingo	*doo-**meen**-goo*